THE ABUSERS

THE ABUSERS

by GARY FISHER
with Robert L. McGrath

mott media
BOX 236, MILFORD, MI. 48042

All Scriptures are from the King James Version of the Bible

Some of the names in this book have been changed to protect the individuals involved. The events are absolutely as described.

Printed in the United States of America
Library of Congress Catalog Card Number: 74-27322
ISBN: Hardcover 0-915134-04-7   Softcover Trade 0-915134-05-5
HV 742.C2 F 57

DEDICATED TO
my father-in-law and mother-in-law,
Percy and Louise Jones.
When I was a nobody,
they treated me like I was a somebody,
and to the greatest wife, Nanell,
and children, Shane and Sherry,
a man could ever have.

Acknowledgements

My sincere thanks to these people who have helped make this book a reality: Kathy Burkhardt; Ernest E. Ainslie, M.D.; Robert L. McGrath; Peggy Givens, R.N.; Art Linkletter; Randy and Linda Burkes; Percy and Louise Jones; Ralph Coker; Andrae Crouch; Steve and Linda Smith; Mr. and Mrs. Bean and all the Kids at Sylmar Solid Rock Coffee House; Mom Taylor and Kids; Ron and Janie Chapman; Dave and Marilyn Woods; Jene Wilson and Family; Joe King and Family; Mrs. Helen Dewey and her son, Daryl; Lt. Commander Earl Fisher and Family; and Dave Balsiger.

G.F.

Introduction

For several years, I have been aware of the increasing impact generated by the ministry of a young evangelist, the Reverend Gary Fisher of Anaheim, California.

I first came to know Gary Fisher because of my own intense personal interest in seeking solutions to the problems of drug addiction among the youth of our nation. When one of your own has been affected by this insidious evil, you cannot help but pursue every possible avenue to destroy it. I cannot, of course, bring my daughter back, but if I can point the way to truth about drugs for others — young and old alike — I will have achieved a vitally important goal.

That's why I am so enthusiastic over Gary Fisher's life story, *The Abusers*. If ever the atrocities of drug abuse were pinpointed, it is in this gripping narrative of how an abused child developed into an abused man, to the point where the only remaining hope was but a thin thread of faith in the hearts of those who knew this total transgressor. You will marvel, as I did, that Gary Fisher is alive today to transmit the message of the gospel of Jesus Christ.

That he has been an effective messenger for the good of those who hear him is evident not only in the scope of his work today, but also in the latter pages of this book. Yet, through all his tribulations, you'll find a sprinkling of good humor . . . despite the almost insurmountable obstacles facing him, Gary Fisher has triumphed over the evil that abounded in his life, and the true story of that triumph is fascinating reading, indeed.

There have been many successful books written in recent years by rehabilitated drug addicts and by others whose interests have led them to share their knowledge of the problems our society faces, including my own *Drugs At My Doorstep*. But few of those books cover the broad spectrum of human misconduct and suffering you'll find described in *The Abusers*. And the knowledge that great good has risen from the exceeding bad in Gary Fisher's life provides hope for all that there is an answer to every problem . . . if we only know where to find it.

The abused . . . the abuser . . . the fortunate uninvolved onlooker — all can benefit from Gary Fisher's unique life story detailed in these pages.

Art Linkletter

Foreword

I have written introductions for a number of books based on the experiences of other human beings who, like me, have gone through bitter times. I have seen for myself a lot of instances of the amazing change that occurs when the power of God moves in someone's life.

Gary Fisher has an exciting story to tell. Like many others that I have known, Gary's addiction to drugs and alcohol seemed hopeless. He underwent abuse of the body and mind over a long period of time — from childhood until close to the age of 30 years.

Exposing this kind of treatment to public view as Gary does in his life story is an act of courage, making *The Abusers* one of the most important books yet published to prove the power of God's love.

If you had known Gary Fisher as I did — when he was troubled, confused, reaching out for guidance but unable to use it when it was offered — you would recognize the miracle that occurred in his life. I am proud to be his friend, to know that his influence for good is broadening day by day. What the Lord did for Gary Fisher, He can do for you . . . for all His children.

I am happy to recommend *The Abusers* as a true account of one of the most amazing histories of human suffering and evil ever recorded. You won't forget it!

Nicky Cruz

Preface

I first met Gary Fisher when he came to Teen Challenge in Los Angeles a number of years ago. He was at that time the victim of a strife-torn life that had seen him conduct a futile search for a reality he knew must exist somewhere, but was unable to find. Plagued with a background of child neglect and abuse, alcoholism, drug addiction, jail and mental hospital abuse, and other troubles, this young man carried problems enough for twenty people. He had already attempted suicide repeatedly. And where Teen Challenge was concerned, he was a three-time loser — a fence-straddler, guilty of "using" the Teen Challenge program by pretending to follow its precepts, but at the same time rejecting its basic principle that love of the Lord Jesus Christ is the truth that sets us free.

I am humbly thankful to God that when Gary Fisher's life was finally turned around to total commitment to the Master, my own prayers and faith in him as a fellow human being may have played some small part in his rebirth in Christ.

To me, it is amazing that so many tribulations could be visited upon one individual, and yet those same trials have produced a person whose love of the Lord has already brought new hope and faith to thousands of people of all ages. And I am sure this is only the beginning.

Andrae Crouch

THE ABUSERS

Chapter One

That night I looked at my face in the bathroom mirror, drew back my fist, listened for a moment to the drunken quarreling of my mother and stepfather in the other room, and then swung with all my strength. Glass shattered in all directions, which surprised me more than anything else; I was only seven years old.

But I had finally had it. Night after night, that summer of 1946, my parents had totally ignored me to give the bottle their undivided attention, and in desperation I'd have done anything to get them to pay some attention to me.

When nothing happened, I wound a handkerchief around my bleeding fingers, went into the next room and announced I was going to run away from home. I thought that would make them feel bad, maybe even sorry for me.

"Fine," my stepfather said, taking another drink, "let me help you pack."

He went into the bedroom and found a big white canvas seabag my dad had owned, and tossed all my clothes into it. My stepfather even carried the bag down the stairs and out the front door of the ancient hotel where we lived on Bunker Hill in Los Angeles. It was the most attention he'd given me in weeks.

"Goodbye, Gary," he said, patting me on the back. "Good luck!"

I guess he was glad to see me go, although he was so drunk he probably didn't really know what he was doing. And my mom didn't pay any attention at all, because she'd already passed

1

out. She'd had plenty of time, because it was already 10:30.

I wandered slowly down the street, dragging the bag along. I knew what I wanted to do, but I wasn't sure how to do it. I wanted to find my real father, but I knew he'd only be drinking somewhere. I was fairly well acquainted, though, where some of the bars were, and I began checking them out, one by one.

My fingers hurt where I'd cut them, so I had to drag the seabag with my left hand. And for some reason, all the buildings along the street and the neon signs and the street lights and cars and everything looked twice as big as I remembered them in daylight. All I'd wanted was some attention. I blinked to hold back the tears and shoved at the door to a bar. I hoped — desperately — that this would be the right place, that my dad would be inside.

"Hey, kid, what're you doing here?" The voice was gravelly and loud. It had to be loud to carry over the noise in that people-packed place. I'd been scared, outside; I was petrified, here.

"I'm looking for Fred Fisher," I squeaked. "He's my dad."

The gravelly voice softened a little. "Yeah, I know him," the bartender said. "Ain't seen him tonight."

"Oh." I wasn't really surprised. I'd never been lucky in all my seven years, so why should that change now? I turned to go.

"Try the Lucky Seven, down the next block," a voice said. "Fred goes in there quite a bit, I think."

"Thanks," I nodded, dragging the seabag out the door. "I'll go see."

I tried to keep my knees from shaking as I went stumbling along the street. At the Lucky Seven, I got the same answer. They knew my dad, but he hadn't been there that night. But there was a woman there who wanted to help. "He might be at Pat's Place," she said, kneeling down so her face was level with mine, her voice raised to carry over the jukebox.

"That the one with the owl in the window?" I asked, and she nodded. "Been there," I said. "He wasn't there."

"Honey, you shouldn't be out wandering around in the middle of the night!" She put her hand on my shoulder. "You want me to call a couple of places where your daddy might be?"

I thought about it. If my dad wasn't here, I didn't want to

stay here. This woman had been drinking, too, and all of a sudden I just wanted to get out of there.

"No, thank you," I told her, and because I was afraid she'd try to keep me inside with all that racket, I lied a little. "I think I know where he is," I said, and I dragged my bag after me out the door.

There was another bar I knew about on the other side of the street, so I waited till there weren't any cars going either direction and hurried across as fast as I could move. At the entrance, I hesitated. I could feel tears welling up, and I wasn't sure I could stand it if I didn't find my dad here.

Slowly I walked inside. There wasn't any door on the place, just a crooked hallway. It was dark, and I stood there waiting for my eyes to adjust. Then I saw him!

I dropped the bag and ran to the table where my father sat, holding a glass with both hands. "Daddy!"

He jumped and knocked the glass over, but neither of us paid any attention. "Gary! What are you doing here?"

He took my hand, and suddenly everything was all right again. Dad would look after me. I knew it!

"They kicked me out of the hotel," I said grinning. "So I have to live with you now, right?"

My dad looked at me for a long time, right in my eyes. Then he slowly shook his head. "No, Son," he said. "I'm afraid I just don't have a place where I can keep you. I've got to be gone all day." He reached out and set his glass back up straight on the table and stared at it while I stood there and clung to his other hand. "I reckon we better go back there and straighten this out," he said then. "Come on, Son."

My throat suddenly cramped. This wasn't working out at all! The hard edge to the tone of his "come on" frightened me. I knew my dad well enough to know some of his feelings.

The way he snatched up the bottle from the floor beside his chair as we started to leave made it even more evident that he was working up to a fit of anger.

"Do we have to go back there, Daddy?" I pleaded, hoping somehow I could change the way things were going.

He grabbed my arm. "Come on!" he said. I stopped at the

doorway to pick up my bag, but he took it away from me, still holding the bottle in his other hand. I had to run to keep up with him as he headed up the street toward the hotel.

When we arrived, dad began to yell up toward the second-story window where our rooms were.

"Come on down here, you miserable —" he called, using some foul names. "I'm going to tear your stinking head off!"

My stepfather stuck his head out of the window. "All right, Curly," he said, using my father's nickname. "You put that bottle down, and I'll come down."

So dad set the bottle down and waited while I stood there and shivered. There was a big knot in my stomach, and another one in my throat. I didn't know which way to turn. I wanted to be loved; I wanted to live with my dad who might pay some attention to me, and here I was with my dad and my stepfather ready to take each other apart.

Just then, my stepfather burst out the front door of the hotel. He had a bottle of his own in one hand and I couldn't see the other. He ran up to dad, and then I saw it.

"Daddy!" I yelled. "Look out!"

It was too late. My stepfather had a small galvanized garbage bucket in the hand he'd held behind his back, and with one quick swing, he smashed it on my dad's head. He crumpled to the ground with blood streaming over the side of his face, and I fell on top of him, crying. I think that may have kept my stepfather from hitting him again, because when I looked up he was just standing there like he didn't know what he'd done.

I hated my stepfather then and would have killed him if I could. But I was crying so hard I couldn't think of anything to do except get help. So I got up and ran to the 24-hour restaurant next door and asked someone there to call an ambulance. The next thing I remembered was the ambulance taking my dad away. I wished I had a gun, so I could shoot my stepfather.

A close relative has verified the problems, which I don't remember, but were created in my earlier years by my alcoholic parents. In a written statement to me, she cites time after time when their neglect became child abuse. When I was six months old, for example, a neighbor informed her that I was on my parent's front porch, clad only in a diaper, and that she had been unable to arouse my parents. My relative found me there asleep, and because my parents were drunk, took me home with her. Three or four days later, my father came after me; they'd known where I was, according to her, but "were having too good a time to be bothered. . ."

After that, she kept watch on my parents' behavior and neglect. Many nights, she states, they would go to bars and drink until closing time, leaving me in a locked auto. On weekends she would visit their home, often finding me in pajamas at late afternoon, the only food available being some bologna still in its wrapper, or perhaps a dill pickle; but there was plenty of booze on hand.

At 19 months, with my father seriously ill in the hospital, I was playing in the street and hit by a car, remaining unconscious for several hours while police searched vainly for my mother. They finally reached my relative at work, and she rushed to the hospital to sign for possible emergency surgery. Another relative finally located my mother hiding under the bed at home, "very much out of it" from alcohol.

Not long afterward, my relative received a frantic call from my father. He said my mother had run off, taking everything but me, and would she please come and get me. They had moved some distance away, to Tarzana, but she drove there only to find me all alone in a locked shack they called home. My father was nowhere in sight, and she had to climb through a window to get me. The place was bare; I had on a romper, no underwear, no shoes, and there was nothing to eat — only a nearly empty bottle of orange drink with mold on it. It took her a week or more to get the splinters out of my feet, legs and bottom.

This relative wanted to believe my parents' continuing promises that "this time we'll take good care of him." It never happened; to this day, my dear relative feels she was remiss in not demanding that I be placed permanently in her custody. At that time, my brother was frequently cared for by another relative so there was a distinct difference in our early backgrounds.

Getting back to the times I remember, it wasn't only my

mother and father or, later on, my stepfather that terrified me; they seemed to attract all the other alcoholics in the neighborhood. In fact, the old hotel was usually full of them; they wandered in and out of our rooms and theirs like it was just a big family house.

I would rub their backs for them, and they'd give me a nickel, a dime, or sometimes even a quarter. It was a good way to hustle bubble gum money. Once I went into a room to rub a guy's back — he was a friend of my mother's — and I rubbed him for about an hour before I realized . . . he was dead! Death was a frequent visitor there, but that particular time really got to me.

Then there were the parties. I'd stay up till three in the morning, playing my one-string guitar, while the drunks around me would sing old songs like "Red River Valley," and throw pennies on the floor for me. Drunks were always there — crying and fighting and vomiting on the floor and in the bed and in the kitchen and out the window. The stench of it made me sick to my stomach, but I couldn't do a thing about it.

One time my father was lying on the shabby old couch in our living room in the hotel; all of a sudden we realized it was afire. It was three in the morning, and we had quite a time getting everyone out of the hotel, so many were in one sort of stupor or another. The couch completely burned, and everything in our apartment was smoked up pretty badly, but no one was hurt. My dad and the rest of the drunks were always burning holes in the rug and the couch; it's a wonder we weren't all cremated.

Apprehension was my prevailing mood in those early years. It wasn't only fear of the alcoholics around me all the time, it was the gangs that roamed the Echo Park area of Los Angeles, too. There were several bands of them, and when they weren't planning a rumble with a rival gang, they were always ready to take apart any stray kids who might stumble into their territory. I used to walk two or three miles out of my way, going to the Villa Heights Elementary School, because I was afraid one of the gangs would take my lunch money away from me. And quite often, they'd get it anyway.

Most of them were Mexicans — we called them Pachucos — and there were always four or five of them. I wasn't afraid to

fight, but there wasn't much use trying to take on that many —
especially when they were bigger than me anyway.

Most of my contact with adults was limited to a particular
type of person. And because of that I remember attending many
Alcoholics Anonymous meetings with my mother. I always
enjoyed the meetings, but I especially liked the AA dances.
Mother would put me on her toes and dance me around the floor.
But I might end up that same night rubbing the back of some
poor outcast who'd let the lure of the bottle take control again.

* * * *

Eventually my mother and stepfather decided they couldn't
handle my older brother Earl, who was nicknamed Bud, and me
any longer, so they put us in a home for boys. Maybe they did it
out of love for us, knowing they were incapable of providing any
kind of a home for two children. But all they actually did was
move us from one atmosphere of fear to another. We were there
for nearly four years, and every Friday was whipping day. I
couldn't seem to stay out of trouble, so Friday was something to
dread.

I didn't understand why I couldn't be at home with my mom,
bottle or not. It was better there, and I resented having to be
cooped up in a home with a lot of other kids. So we spent our
time finding new ways to make trouble. It was, I suppose, one
way of getting the attention we all wanted and needed. It wasn't
love, but at least it was attention.

For instance, there was one crazy stunt we used to always
pull because the boys' home was next door to an old ladies'
home. We'd go out on the back fire escape and strip down naked
and run yelling around the old ladies' home.

We would try to get back in without getting caught, but it
seemed like I was always the one who got nabbed. Along with
me, there was a boy named Alex and another we called Wienie
Dog, and invariably, come Friday, we'd be shoved into a closet
and they'd get their special board and whip us good.

The woman who dished out the whippings must have
weighed three hundred pounds. "All right, drop your pants!"
she would say. "Grab that hook over your head and hang on!"

Then she'd start swinging, really whaling me with that board, often missing my rear and hitting my legs and back till I couldn't hang on to the hook any longer, and I would fall to the floor. It didn't make me scared, and it sure didn't make me sorry. It just made me hate everything around me all the more.

When I think of what went on in that place, I shudder. A lot of the kids, including my brother and me, had lice in their hair. We couldn't help it — they were all around us. What's more, we slept four in a bed and everyone of us, but my brother, was a bed-wetter. And we didn't eat well at all. Only once in a great while did we have any meat.

There was a little Mexican boy who lived in the neighborhood who obviously had troubles, too, and I would try to save up food for him. He'd often come climbing over the back fence, and up to the cafeteria where we ate, and at the risk of an extra whipping, I'd give him some bread or something through the window by lifting up the screen.

On Sundays we would line up and march about a mile to a huge, barn-like church. When we walked through the door we would put our hands into a bowl of water and everyone would do some motions with their hands before walking on in to sit down. The pastor would come out and talk in a language we couldn't understand. Then he would bless us and send us home, and when I got there, I didn't know anything more than when we started.

My mother would come to visit us on weekends, and we'd take our fifteen cents weekly allowance and go with her to the corner drug store to buy a banana split. What a treat that was! When she'd leave us again, it would break our hearts.

My father's visits were a highlight, too. He would come and take Bud and me out to lunch or dinner, and buy us little hats and stuff. For a short while, it would be like God Himself had come to take us for a walk and we'd think we were in heaven. I loved my father, despite his faults, and I just couldn't understand why we couldn't be together more. And when he had to go, it was almost more than I could stand.

But the day finally came when my mother and stepfather drove up in a beautiful, new, blue Ford convertible, ready to take us to live with them once more. It was like seeing angels in a heavenly chariot and the car indicated my stepfather had been on the wagon long enough to start making good money again, which he always seemed to be able to do when he was sober. Then, desperation for me.

"We can't let Gary go with you," the manager said. "He is a bad one and has to stay because he needs discipline!"

My heart sank. I knew I was bad, but the main reason I acted the way I did was because I wanted so much to go home.

"He's our son," my mother said with quiet authority. I'd never heard her speak so firmly. "He's going with us!"

The manager shrugged. "All right, I guess he's your problem. Lots of luck!"

My mom may not have known it, but she would need lots of luck with me around. I'd learned a great deal in that home for boys, and it didn't take long to turn what I'd learned into heavier problems for my parents. As we drove away from the home, I turned for a last, hate-filled look. I did not know then that it was only the first of many institutions I would endure, and not the worst by any means.

Chapter Two

When you're lonely and looking for someone to love you, you reach out in every possible way — you extend your own love in hopes of getting love back in return. But there were lessons to be learned about loving, about human nature, and I learned them the hard way.

A frequent visitor to our house was a German fellow — really a pleasant man, and I took an instant liking to him, because he seemed interested in me. Wanting to be loved, I opened my heart to Hans, and I felt as if I'd finally found a friend.

I guess my mother and stepfather thought so, too, because they left him with me in the house one night, while they and Bud went to the movies. Hans had been drinking, but there was nothing unusual about that — it was part of the daily scene.

We had an old television set — one of the early ones with a very small screen. Hans and I were watching it, trying to follow the somewhat blurred action on the eleven inch tube.

"Gary," Hans said to me with a grin, "I'm getting hungry. How about you?"

"Yeah," I said, and because I wanted to do whatever I could for Hans, I went into the kitchen to see what I could find to give him. There wasn't anything in the refrigerator except beer. At eleven years old I wasn't much of a cook, but I looked around and found a can of spaghetti, which I opened, heated on the stove, and put on a plate for him.

When I started to set it on the table in front of Hans, he reached out as if he were going to pat me on the back — except it wasn't my back he was reaching for. A chill of fright shook me, and I dropped the plate and took off running. I had no idea why Hans had grabbed at me that way, but I knew it was something very wrong and I wanted to get away from him fast.

I scooted into my mother's room, slid under the bed, and managed to pull a small rug over me, only moments before I heard Hans' heavy step.

"Gary!" he yelled. "Where are you?"

I lay there shaking, and couldn't have forced a sound from my lips if I'd wanted to.

"Gary! Wherever you are, come out!" There was a wild desperation in Hans' hoarse voice — a tone that turned him into the wolf-man or Frankenstein's monster or a creature from outer space. I wished bitterly I could dig a hole in the floor, but I could only lie there beneath the rug and hold my mouth open to keep my teeth from clattering.

I could hear Hans' steps, moving slowly around the bed. "Gary! Come out, Gary!" It was a wild scream, the voice of a madman.

Then, *crash*, and a tinkle of glass. He had broken the window in the den next to the bedroom in his fury to find me. "Gary — come out now!"

I lay there, unable to breathe, grateful to hear those heavy footfalls retreat down the hall. But I dared not move. I sensed, without really knowing why, that my life was in the balance.

Another crash, followed by the tinkling of glass, and I knew another window was gone. How I wished for someone to come to the house! I'd never been afraid of grown men before, except for my stepfather and once in a while, my dad. But never before had I felt this hopeless panic. His screams from the other room froze me to the floor.

"All right, Gary, the game's over." The voice was softer now, wheedling, the words slurred by a thickened tongue. "You can come out, Gary. No more hide-and-seek. That's a nice boy!"

I stayed put. I could hear his voice from the other room, winding down like a turned-off phonograph record. "Gary . . . Gary . . . Gary . . ."

After what seemed an age, I heard the front door open, and

only then did I roll out from under the rug and the bed. Hans, I saw, had gone to sleep in the chair in the living room. And mom and my stepfather and Bud were chattering away, hardly noticing him.

Haltingly, I told them what had happened, but I could tell they didn't believe me. My stepfather pointed to the forlorn figure sprawled in the chair, snoring fitfully.

"He sure looks dangerous!" he grinned.

"He is!" I shouted, not caring now if Hans woke up.

"All right, Gary!" my mother soothed. "We'll take care of it."

But all they did was look at each other and shake their heads. Even if they believed me, I'm sure there were two reasons why they didn't take any action: they probably felt compassion for Hans, a fellow-alcoholic who might logically have lost normal control, and they probably didn't know what to do. So they wound up doing nothing.

Next morning, though, my stepfather did take me for a walk. "Gary," he said, stopping and looking at me, "there's something you should know, about what happened last night," and I was grateful that at least they finally believed what I'd said.

I nodded. Any action or explanation would be appreciated. I only knew I'd been scared to death.

"Hans is a sick man," my stepfather said. "He's — mixed up. He probably wouldn't have tried to hurt you, except he was drunk."

He paused, searching for the right words. "We have to try to help people who are sick, Gary," he said. "We have to try to understand they need help — and not blame them or turn them aside."

I was pleased my stepfather was taking the time to have a man-to-man talk with me, but I was disappointed at the sum total of what he had to say. Anyway, from that time forth, I was very careful about giving my friendship to older men.

* * * *

My hands were constantly scarred from fist fights with whatever I ran into — Bud, other boys, trees, telephone poles, walls, street lights, parking meters . . . I would strike out in anger and frustration at them all. Because I couldn't get back at my stepfather for the drunken mistreatments he dished out, I took out my frustration on whatever was nearest me. I had a mean streak in me that wouldn't quit.

I was used to gangs, of course. I grew up knowing they were always lurking in the background, ready to pounce on me or any unsuspecting youngster they could extort a few pennies from, or else subject to tortures, just for the fun of it. And though I'd made friends with some of the Pachucos, they seemed to be the ones I'd usually get into fights with.

When I reached the sixth grade, I was at a new school in Redondo Beach, and within a short time, I managed to get off on the wrong foot. I walloped a Mexican boy square in the mouth one day, and right after school, he and four others were laying for me. I managed to outrun them, over the hills, past the city dump, through "Mexican-town," and I was home free.

That wasn't the end of it, though. That night, I went to the school gymnasium with my stepfather for a Boy Scout meeting. He was doing his best to give Earl and me a decent life like other boys enjoyed. I looked out the window and twenty-five or thirty Mexicans were waiting for me. I had no choice but to tell my stepfather of the earlier incident.

He listened soberly while I explained what had happened, probably stretching the truth a little as to why I'd hit the other boy in the mouth that day.

"Okay," he said. "Let's go!"

We went out together, and my stepfather didn't flinch as we walked up to the menacing group. "All right," he said, "who's the one who wants to fight my son?"

A boy about my size stepped forward, and we went at it. I don't know if either one of us really won the fight, but when we'd each managed to get in some pretty good blows, the group seemed to be satisfied, and off they went. In school, they left me alone for quite a while after that.

Hitting the Mexican boy was just one of the things I did that defied logical explanation. If there was any way to get into trouble, I'd find it. One day I left school, just looking for a ruckus — something I could get an exciting kick out of, because I was bored, tired of being ignored at home and generally mad at the world around me and everything in it.

I was walking by a lady's house where there was a beautiful, well-trimmed hedge all across the front of the yard. I leaped into the hedge, and began trampling it down to nothing. The urge to destroy, something I was to experience with increasing frequency as I grew older, simply overtook me.

The lady discovered me, and rushed out her front door screaming. I couldn't make out what she was saying, but there wasn't any need to. I took off running, with her chasing me down the street. I didn't stop until I got home.

"Dad!" I said breathlessly, "there's an old lady after me. She thinks I jumped into her hedge, but it wasn't me — it was another guy. She's all mixed up!"

Suddenly there was a loud pounding on the front door, and my stepfather opened it to see this terribly angry woman stamping her foot, still screaming almost incoherently.

"Now just a minute," my stepfather said quietly. "My son just told me he didn't jump into your hedge, and he doesn't lie. You'd better just go on back home and cool off."

She stood there stunned, and glared at him, while he stared back at her. Then she turned and went back down the street, shaking her head and muttering to herself.

I was amazed at how easily and effectively he had gotten me out of a really bad situation, and after that, lying became increasingly a part of my life.

There were times when I was caught and disciplined, of course, both as a youngster and later in life. One time I begged my stepfather to buy me a bow and arrow. He finally agreed, only after I promised never to point it at anyone.

"I promise!" I said.

So I played with my bow and arrow, and everything was great. But along came a young lady riding a horse, and I imagined I was a fierce Indian and she was a cowboy, and checking to make sure my stepfather wasn't looking, I pulled back on the bow and aimed the arrow at the "cowboy." It was just a game; I wasn't really going to shoot her.

But the moment I pulled back on the bow, out of the corner of my eye, I saw my stepfather coming, so I took off running down the street. I had no idea he could run so fast for such a short little guy. In less than a block, he caught up, tackled me, and the licking I got wasn't soon forgotten. Even though I had it coming, I resented it, and the perverse streak that seemed to be part of me got worse instead of better.

It came out in many ways, most graphically in the things I did to animals. Whenever I got my hands on something — alive or dead — I felt a compulsion to squeeze it. I would even stand over my brother's bed when he was asleep and wonder what would happen if I squeezed his throat between my hands. I didn't dare squeeze him when he was asleep, but I often thought of doing it. I would sometimes squeeze clay, imagining it was someone's neck I was holding.

I kept about thirty hamsters in a shed behind the house, and when I'd become so filled with hate at my stepfather for his mistreatment of my mother, my brother, and me, I'd take it out on my hamsters, sometimes actually squeezing them to death.

I even fastened a big firecracker to the back of a cat one time, then lit it and let the poor animal run. When the firecracker exploded, it blew part of the cat's backside away. I decided I'd better do away with the evidence of my misdoings, so I dug a hole and buried the cat alive.

In the house, thinking about it, I was afraid the cat might get out of its grave, so I dug it up — it was still breathing — and with the shovel I pounded out of it what life it had left.

* * * *

Life was better as I approached my teenage era. My step-father, a brilliant man gone wrong on booze, was making good money in the lumber business, and that made things easy. He built us a lovely home in Redondo Beach, and in the times when he wasn't drinking, everything was fine. But those times were still far too few, and of short duration.

He couldn't seem to stand prosperity, so he'd go on a binge and end up beating my mother and blacking out himself. She'd often end up with ebony eyes and a broken nose, her face brutally smashed. Then he'd lose his business, and we'd go through the whole thing again. Sober, he was a fantastic operator; drunk, he was one of the meanest men who ever lived.

Ironically enough, even though I could see the horrors of alcoholism around me constantly, my goal in life was trying the same thing. We'd go surfing at the beach all the time, and when we weren't there, we'd be out behind the piles of redwood at my stepfather's lumberyard, smoking cigarettes. I learned how to smoke at the age of twelve — thinking I was a pretty big man. I'd usually hide behind the house, out by my hamster shed, and smoke the cigarettes I'd stolen from my mom.

At the beach, our biggest aim was to get drunk, and it was easy to do. We'd walk to the beach, collecting all the wine and whiskey bottles we could find on the way, pouring what was left in them into one big bottle. By the time we got to the beach, we'd have a bottleful of every kind of drink you could imagine. It didn't take much to get smashed on that deadly combination, but the next day, my head would feel like it was going to split in two and go into orbit by itself. It was a kind of drinking that could have killed us, and it's a wonder it didn't.

By my twelfth year I was so hardened in my rebellion that in school I was considered a "non-achiever" — not an under-achiever. It meant I was such a hopeless incorrigible that the teachers, the school, everyone, had simply given up on me.

A newspaper headline caught my eye not long ago. It read: *Half of Graduates at Four High Schools Called Inept Readers.* I could predict what it said even before reading the article. It briefly stated that "more than half of the students in four high school graduating classes studied by the 1973-74 Los Angeles Grand Jury were practically unable to read . . . tests also revealed only one out of five seniors at the four schools were able to read at 'acceptable levels.' "*

It could have been written about me, for in all the years I was sent to school, I never learned to read. I was pushed up to the next level at the end of each year until I finally became a dropout

Copyright, 1974, Los Angeles Times. Reprinted by permission.

without even completing my freshman year in high school. In reality, I probably never actually "completed" the third grade. But because I was a non-achiever — a child who rebelled against discipline and other classroom rigors — I was constantly shoved aside and ignored. Lacking attention, I concentrated on making trouble, meantime learning nothing.

The article went on to state, "It is practically impossible to teach a child to read or get his cooperation when that child's parents are indifferent or antagonistic toward the schools and teachers." Steeped in alcohol, my parents were both indifferent and antagonistic, depending on how they happened to feel at a given moment.

But the article also pointed out that another part of the problem "originates from those teachers and administrators who lack ability, tact, and understanding." Abuse of our children's education today remains a reality, one that all of us need to lend some serious attention.

It was bad enough to have to face alcoholic parents daily but then I learned about one of my seventh grade teachers. She often returned to the classroom after lunch with the glassy-eyed look an alcoholic usually gets, a look I knew well.

If I learned little at school, I was learning a lot about alcoholism. I planned to avoid such a fate and make sure it wouldn't happen to me. Even when I would see my stepfather at his most senseless state — when he would take me on a drunken spree to Las Vegas and flush $50 bills down the toilet just to show off — I still thought I could rise above all that, it would never happen to me.

Chapter Three

At length, my mother and stepfather came to the end of their rope. Finding themselves unable to cope with me — at fourteen I was constantly getting drunk, getting into trouble at school, picking fights with anyone in my way — my parents decided to give my father and his wife a try.

Only a short time after I'd gone to live with them, I pulled a crazy stunt that showed I was willing to try anything to get someone to feel sorry for me and love me. I took a razor blade and slashed myself on the face and stomach. Then I stumbled in off the street and told my dad that a gang had jumped me and stabbed me and cut me up. He didn't know it, of course, but all I wanted was some sympathy and attention. He was concerned for about fifteen minutes, then he had more important things to do.

I could not get along with my father's wife at all and would whistle incessantly, just to provoke her. Once I knew it was a weak spot with her, I played it for all it was worth.

"Stop that infernal whistling!" she would shout at me.

"Sure," I'd say, and then as soon as her back was turned, I'd start whistling again, softly at first, so maybe she could barely hear it, and then getting gradually louder, just to see what would happen. It was one way to get attention, a wrong way, of course.

"I just can't put up with that whistling any more!" she'd tell my dad, and he'd land on me.

"Gary, knock it off! I mean it!" he'd say, and I'd look as innocent as could be.

"Sure, Dad," I'd say, looking a little hurt, and as soon as he

18

was gone, I'd start in again. I did it so often, I sometimes didn't realize myself that I was whistling.

One day at breakfast, in early May, 1954, I'd been whistling before we sat down, and once seated, he let me have it.

"Gary, what have I told you about that hellish whistling?" he began, and this time, for some reason, it really rubbed me the wrong way.

I didn't say a word. I just reached under the breakfast table, took hold of the edge, and suddenly lifted it up in the air, dumping bacon and eggs and toast and coffee and everything else right on top of both of them.

That capped it, of course. I could see fire leaping out of my dad's eyes, so I took off through the back door and jumped over the six steps to the ground with him hot on my trail. I spun around the backyard, and vaulted a five-foot chain link fence. There was a gate, but I didn't have time to use it.

Dad was right at my heels, but he didn't make the fence, and I kept right on running. I don't know why, but I went on to school. It's a wonder I didn't run away the rest of the day, but after school, I came home and hid under the front steps for well over an hour. I could hear my dad walking up and down those steps, and I knew he was just waiting for me to show up.

Finally, I figured I had to face it some time, so I sneaked out from under the steps and slipped inside the house to the bathroom, but I didn't lock it, and the minute I flushed the toilet, he yanked open the door.

"I'm sorry, Dad," I blurted, hoping to save myself a strapping. "I didn't mean to do it." What a whopper! How could somebody 'accidentally' overturn a table?

But to my surprise, he said calmly, "Come on in here, Gary; I want to talk to you."

So I followed him into the living room, wondering what was coming up now.

"Son," my dad said, "you're going to have to finish school and do right, and you're just not cutting it."

I nodded. I loved having my father — or anyone else — talk straight to me. It happened so seldom, I even enjoyed it when I was getting chewed out.

"We've called your mother," Dad said then, "and we've decided the best thing to do is send you to The Hacienda."

"Great!" I said. "Is that some kind of ranch or academy where I can learn to ride a horse or box and things like that?"

He shook his head. "Well, not exactly," he said. "It's a place where you can get the kind of help you need, finish school and make something of yourself."

It sounded fine to me. "When do I go?" I asked.

"Your mother will pick you up tomorrow at noon and take you there." He paused. "And if I hear you whistle one more time between now and then, I'll wallop the daylights out of you!"

I heard him loud and clear. I clamped my lips together, and I didn't whistle a note, not until I saw the layout at The Hacienda the next afternoon — and by then it was too late to whistle.

Nestled in the hills near Riverside, the administration building and the garage and the dormitories gave me a sort of eerie feeling, as we drove up to them. "The Hacienda — Since 1907" was on the sign at the entrance, and some of the buildings looked like they'd been there all that time. Others were newer, and I could see from the well-kept grounds and the rolling farmland around them that someone had done a lot of work here. I had a strange feeling I knew who had done that work, and I knew I didn't want any part of it. But I went through the motions of accepting it when my mother took me in and introduced me to the superintendent and the other people in charge.

"You'll like it here, Gary," one of the men said. "We have a football team and a swimming pool, and all kinds of things." Then he said something I didn't like at all.

"Gary will be assigned a number," he said to my mother. "It will be his identification here at The Hacienda. He'll be Number 4502."

I remembered an old movie I'd seen about convicts in striped clothes, each with a number. I wondered when they'd bring me my striped suit. I didn't wait for them to hang my number on me or to find out about the football team and the swimming pool. The minute my mother drove out the driveway I went over the hill. They might want to put me in jail, but until they locked me up, I wasn't about to stay.

I walked a long way in the nearby river bed, and then managed to hitchhike back to Redondo Beach, but I didn't go home. Instead, I looked up a friend of mine, an Italian boy I called Wop. He had a big Cadillac, and we'd gone party crashing quite a few times, getting drunk and starting fights and staying out all night whooping it up. He wasn't too surprised to see me.

"Where you been, Gary?" he asked, and when I told him, he shook his head. "That's not for you, man! Let's find a party tonight and have a blast. That's the only way to fly."

But three days later, I decided I'd better call my mom, and before I knew it, she had spirited me straight back to The Hacienda. After all, she and my dad had to pay to get them to keep me there, so I couldn't really blame her. The people in charge weren't so friendly this time, and I decided I'd cool it a while before pulling the pin again. There seemed to be nothing else to do but "get into the program," so I stayed to see what it was all about.

That first night when I went to bed in Room 13 of Collins Cottage, where I was to live with fifteen other boys, I heard some funny noises. I got up and went out behind the cottage and found a bunch of the guys putting plastic bags over their faces.

"What's the scene?" I said, trying to talk big.

"It's a gas, man!" one of the boys said. "Here — try a whiff."

They were glue-sniffing, I realized, and I thought, what the heck, there's nothing else to do. Maybe this will help me get out of the bog of loneliness and bitterness I'm in.

So I pulled the plastic bag over my face and took a big drag at it; my head popped and I wasn't worried at all about not being with my family. The glue put me on a high that almost blew my mind. It was the first time I'd flipped out with anything but alcohol; it was an entirely new experience. I felt like my brain had exploded and was now being pasted back together. I couldn't even breathe right, but I felt I was flying around like a bird. That glue was trouble! It was a lot like getting drunk, but just enough different to be more exciting.

I was learning fast at The Hacienda, which was really just a polite name for juvenile hall. The next day, I picked up something else. We went down to the front of the main building and found a truck parked there. First thing I knew, one of the boys had removed the gas cap and stuck his face down against it.

"What's going on?" I asked.

"Try it — you'll like it!" I was told, so I stuck my nose next to the open gas tank, and took a heavy sniff of gasoline. Once again my head started swimming, only with a different sensation than the glue had brought.

"This place isn't bad," I said to myself. "It's got a lot of ways to get away from it all. Who needs a family around? They only give you a hard time anyway." So I did my best to fit into the curriculum, especially the extra-curricular activities of the rest of the boys who shared Collins Cottage with me.

It wasn't easy, but I did have some things going for me. The ringleaders, I found, were just like me — rebellious, mean, nasty, ready to do anything they could to hurt or be cruel to others. It was easy to fit into that scheme, because that description was tailor-made for me at fifteen years of age.

I hadn't been there long when I was assigned to grass crew one day, raking grass in a field that was part of the complex. Everyone in the place had nicknames — mine was "Dead Fish" — and there was a sixteen-year-old called "Blue Boy" who was in charge of running the grass crew.

I needed to go to the bathroom, so I told Blue Boy. "Forget it!" he said. "You keep on raking that grass till I tell you to go!"

I looked at him for a moment, then turned away, laid down my rake, and off I went to the nearest washroom. I didn't even bother to look around. Minutes later, as I was sitting on the toilet, Blue Boy stormed in, and without saying a word, began kicking me — between the legs, on my chest, arms, all over. He had me pinned tight. With my pants down, I couldn't get up to kick back, and he gave me a good lesson in dirty fighting.

Surprisingly enough, we became rather good friends after that. And I discovered one basic fact about correctional facilities and the abuse their inmates learn to expect: Unless you're ready to fight for your life, you don't say you're going to do something when someone in authority says you're not. It was a truth I put to good use many times after that.

You had to be able to fight in order to survive in that place. But I'd been fighting ever since I could walk, starting with my brother and progressing through all the years I'd attended school, and now here I was, busier than ever doing the same thing. For once I was grateful for what I'd learned about fighting back at Redondo Beach High. But now I had to learn a whole new method of fighting — learn it fast and learn it well.

We used to put targets up on the wall, placing them at different levels — as high as a man's face, his chest, or his stomach and groin. Then we'd practice for two or three hours at a time, kicking the wall to see if we could get our foot in the bull's-eye. We fought with our feet, never with our hands.

There were many times when someone would go down in the middle of a heavy fight, and along with solid kicks to the head, the aggressor would try to stomp his foot on his opponent's throat. It's a wonder someone wasn't killed, and while there were serious injuries from time to time, it was all accepted as part of the game.

The Hacienda is famed for its nature wall decor sold throughout the year to help finance the facility. The boys there gather the greenery that goes to make up the decorations — we used to call them pod-picking expeditions. But when we'd stop off at a store somewhere to get some refreshments, it was easy for some of the boys to engage the proprietor in the business of buying soda pop, while others sneaked out with a couple of bottles of whiskey or vodka. And then what a time we'd have!

We'd get loaded on whatever had been stolen, and then slip out at night and do all sorts of crazy things. There was a sheep and cattle pasture nearby, and we'd go there and chase the sheep and try to ride them. We'd get on the cows, too, but they were rougher, and we usually didn't last long on them.

On one such nocturnal trip, we were all whooping it up pretty big, being well-fortified with our alcoholic plunder, feeling our way along because we didn't have flashlights, and wouldn't have dared use them if they'd been available.

One of the boys was nicknamed "Four Eyes" for obvious reasons, and everyone seemed to enjoy picking on him. We were out in the middle of the pasture, and suddenly we heard a rumbling noise — one we recognized from previous experience.

"Look out!" someone yelled. "The bull's coming!"

We took off in high gear, but there was a barbed wire fence we had to get through or under or over. I managed to get through it somehow — I can't remember exactly how — but poor Four Eyes ran right smack into it, and wrapped himself up good. When he finally got untangled, he looked like he was full of holes — scratches everywhere, like an angry woman with long fingernails had gotten hold of him. When we got back that night, Four Eyes was in worse trouble, because the supervisors wanted to know where he got all the scratches, and no one seemed to know — we all clammed up.

In all fairness, it was not, I must point out, the fault of the authorities in charge. They did the best they could, and they undoubtedly did help some kids get straightened out. But so many of the boys had been sent there with records of offenses like car theft, burglary, robbery, and other criminal acts that most of the time it was a losing battle.

There were boys with mental problems, too. Some of them were so depressed, they'd take a razor blade and slice their wrists, then lie there and bleed, hoping someone would find them, and let them out — a hospital or anywhere else was preferable to the treatment they were getting, they felt.

Good times were part of the scene, too. We played football, basketball, baseball, and swam in the pool. We practiced diving, and even had a diving team to compete with others. There were good and bad work assignments, also — one of the things I learned to like was baling hay, because I felt I could really get strong doing that.

I always wanted to be the hero, of course — the one noticed above anyone else. So once when we were practicing football, the coach called for anyone who thought he could block the opposing team's backfield — three guys who were pretty powerful runners.

"Yeah, I can do it!" I boasted. So we practiced our plays, and on the day of the game, I felt pretty big. I was thinking, "Boy, I'm going to knock all three of those dudes down."

So on the first play, I threw my body into them — and they

ran right over me. I had to be carried off the field. That one play ruined my back and ribs so I could hardly walk for quite a spell. It also taught me another lesson: I suddenly realized I wasn't really so tough after all, and that I needed to stop and think before deciding I was the big man.

One of the friends I made at The Hacienda whose last name was Nichols, got out at the age of sixteen, and within a short time, developed a reputation as "the telephone robber." Instead of getting straightened out he went from bad to worse — he'd carry a shotgun into a telephone booth near a gasoline station and dial the station number.

"I got a gun on you," he'd say, "and I want you to take the money and put it on the curb and then get in the restroom and close the door. If you make a move any other way, I'll blast you to kingdom come!"

Then he'd wait for the frightened station operator, looking out the window, to do as he said, and he'd grab the money and take off. Eventually, he was caught, of course, but he pulled that trick on quite a number of service stations before he got sent up.

Another boy named Hassit, a boxer and one of our best fighters — was killed running away from a bank he'd just robbed. Others I knew died of drug overdoses, car accidents while fleeing from the law and in other violent ways. Despite the best efforts of those in charge, those of us bent on remaining incorrigibles usually got our hearts' desire.

I learned to steal, fight dirty, curse, and make trouble if I wasn't already in trouble. And I learned how to get those around me stirred up. Like the time we pulled a miniature riot. It started in sort of a follow-the-leader situation. We'd been sitting in a counselor's room, and he'd been using a tape recorder, letting us act out a riot as though we were convicts — just something to do, giving us the chance to play a different from usual role.

When we got back to our cottage, five or six of us got to thinking how much fun it had been playing with the tape recorder, so I made a suggestion.

"How about us pulling a riot ourselves — a real one! Why not?"

And the guys around me echoed, "Yeah, why not!"

So we barricaded the cottage door with our beds, and began yelling. "Riot time! We want some improvements around here!"

When the bell rang for dinner, all the rest of the boys from the other cottages, and some from ours who were already outside, lined up in front of the mess hall for chow. Naturally some of us weren't there, and our absence was immediately noticed.

The director sent a boy down to get us. "Mister Howell says for you guys to come on down for chow or you're in trouble."

"Tell him to go shove it!" I yelled back. "We're having a riot. We want some things changed around here!"

Shortly Mr. Howell got on the loudspeaker, and laid it out for us loud and clear. "You guys better get over in this chow line now, or you're in trouble," he said. "You get down here pronto, or you're going on restriction for a good long time!"

We looked at each other. Restriction was something we didn't cherish. It was bad enough being stuck in that place most of the time, and restriction meant all the time — no outside visits to our homes, no visitors at the facility. It was something to think about.

But we didn't budge. None of us wanted to make the first move, so we just stayed there, holding our non-violent riot. We watched as the others dutifully padded off to the mess hall.

"Chow's probably lousy tonight, anyway," I said. "Who needs it?"

"Yeah!" one of the others agreed.

Mr. Howell and a couple of the other men headed our way then and told us in no uncertain terms we were to leave that cottage and get down to the mess hall.

We said a few things we shouldn't have, and told them when they met our demands, we'd come out.

"What demands are you talking about?" Mr. Howell asked.

We looked at each other. We hadn't even thought about what our demands ought to be.

"We'll let you know!" I yelled back at him.

They talked briefly, and then walked away, leaving us alone. Within an hour, unable to agree on any worthwhile demands we might make and expect to have granted, we decided to unbarricade the door, and sheepishly made our way to the mess hall. But once there, we discovered what food was left that night was, indeed, pretty bad, so we began banging our spoons on the tables and yelling — rioting again.

Mr. Howell was there almost instantly. "Okay, you're already on restriction. The next boy who makes a peep will stay on restriction for six months!" he announced. "You want to miss going home or getting any weekends away, you just say the word!"

None of us made a sound. I decided the chow wasn't so bad after all, and I tasted it tentatively. The others followed suit. Our riot was at an end, and all we got out of it was three weeks' restriction — but that was far better than six months.

At Christmas, 1954, I went home, and once there, I told my mother I'd had it. "I can't go back there, Mom," I pleaded. "I just can't — it's terrible! I hate it! Please let me stay home!"

"Will you promise to be good and settle down and do right?"

"Oh, yes, Mom — you know I will!" I promised. "I've changed, Mom. I'll really make it this time. Just let me stay home."

So she called The Hacienda and told them I wasn't coming back. Since I hadn't been placed there for any law violation, but rather at the request of my parents and the school authorities, there was no reason why I couldn't be released. I was elated.

The next day, I went to the beach, ran into some old friends, and got drunk. It didn't matter. The alcohol flows freely at Christmastime, and my mother and stepfather tied one on, too. I was back on familiar ground and there would be no Hacienda discipline to stop me now. I could put what I'd learned in that place to work, and life would be just one high after another.

Chapter Four

I realize I've painted an awfully black picture of my early childhood, but there were some shafts of light. I entered the Soapbox Derby once. It happened during one of the infrequent times when my stepfather was sober and industrious, and he not only helped me build my miniature racer, he gave me a lot of moral support. The local Chevrolet garage sponsored me, and I won first place in my first heat in the competition. It was one of the few times I ever won anything, and I could have popped my shirt buttons with pride from the accomplishment.

The second time around I added too much weight to the car, hoping to increase its speed down the track, and it didn't get started rolling quick enough. Even so, the trophy I received for winning the first heat was one of the great events of my younger days. I had been recognized for something other than getting into trouble! It was an exhilarating experience.

Once when I was eleven and interested in the Boy Scouts I wanted to walk the famed Silver Moccasin Trail in the San Bernardino Mountains near Los Angeles. "Gary's too young to make that trek," the Scoutmaster told my parents. "He'll have to wait a year or so."

But my parents could be pretty stubborn when they wanted to, and they knew I wanted to go. Maybe they just wanted to get me out of the house — an entirely understandable attitude. In any case, they prevailed, and the scout leaders finally gave in and allowed me to make the 65-mile, five-day hike with the rest of the older boys.

I not only walked the trail, I carried another boy's pack the last three days; otherwise, he wouldn't have made it. I carried my pack on my back and his on my chest, and once again I felt a surge of pride in accomplishing something worthwhile.

I even made the "Order of the Arrow," one of scouting's most distinguished achievements. And I was just short of becoming an Eagle Scout when the darkness that had dogged me all my life caught up with me once again, and turned my footsteps to other trails leading to devastation.

Yet throughout, there was a surprising balance of good versus bad. I recall one incident where I could easily have gotten way off on the wrong foot, but something kept it from happening.

It came at a time when my mother and stepfather were in one of their periodic sobriety spells. There would be stretches of time when they'd be active in Alcoholics Anonymous, sober as a bench of judges, and extending a needed helping hand to others as unfortunate as they. One of their female friends had come to them for help, hoping to get off the alcoholic binge she'd been indulging in, and they made the mistake of leaving her at the house.

I was in the garage, working on my bicycle, when Ann came out.

"Hi, Gary!" she said warmly. "What are you doing?"

I looked up at her and smiled. I knew about her problems, of course; I'd seen so many human wrecks in my brief span of years that I understood them and felt sorry for them.

"Trying to get this beat-up bicycle to work," I explained. "It's a mess!"

She squatted down beside me, apparently interested in whatever mechanical problem I'd encountered. "Trouble, huh?" she asked.

"Yeah." I pointed a greasy finger at the axle on the back wheel. "I can't seem to get this thing lined up right."

At that moment, her hand found my leg and immediately wandered upwards. Shocked, I was rooted to the spot for a moment, wanting to bolt away as I'd done the time before, when Hans had accosted me. But I couldn't move.

"Gary, you and me — we could have some real fun. How about it?"

There were times when I used to fantasize just such a situation, but now, confronted with the stark reality of it, all I could think of was how to get away. I jumped to my feet, grabbed the upside-down bicycle and turned it rightside up.

"Think I'll give this old bike a try," I said quickly. "Maybe it isn't as bad as I thought."

And before she could do or say anything, I jumped on the bike and pedaled away, even if I couldn't get up much speed because the chain wasn't synchronizing with the axle sprocket the way it should.

In retrospect, the months at The Hacienda were, in some ways, the best of all. The bad things I learned there were not the fault of those in charge, for we did our fighting and wine-drinking and smoking without the knowledge of our supervisors. There were older women — we called them "grannies" — in charge of each of the cottages at The Hacienda, and the extremely firm discipline we needed was difficult for them. Also, our work supervisors and other leaders within the groups had a pretty strong hold over what went on, and as long as we stayed in line in a general way, they didn't interfere with the wrong things we did.

Speaking of leaders within the groups, there was a unique system of keeping everyone in line. Any boy who rocked the boat was simply taken down behind the barn by the other boys in the group and thrashed within an inch of his life. It was crude, even cruel, but it served its purpose. It was discipline — unrefined, of course — and in some ways it constituted abuse, yet it was effective in the over-all interaction of those living at The Hacienda. And if the authorities there knew what was happening, they perhaps wisely, turned the other way. Being disciplined by our peers was more effective than if it had come from the supervisors.

Further on the plus side of the ledger, the place came closer to teaching me how to study than any other school I ever attended — they actually taught me things in their classrooms, and that didn't happen anywhere else.

I even took saxophone lessons, something new and different that I really enjoyed. But there would come times when loneliness would take over, and the first thing I'd know, I'd be over the hill again, thumbing my way back to the Redondo Beach vicinity. I went AWOL a total of three times.

But The Hacienda was just about the last ray of sunshine for a long, long time. After I left, without the restraint and discipline I hated (and never dreamed how badly I needed) I simply went wild.

* * * *

Like the time I wrecked my stepfather's Hudson that he was so proud of. I'd borrowed the car without him knowing it, and I was showing off in it to the two guys I had with me.

I only had a learner's permit at the time, but one of the fellows with me had his license, so I figured I was safe as far as meeting the technical requirement of having a licensed driver with me was concerned. I remember flooring it heading down a hill, and then, horror of horrors! The accelerator stuck, and we were hitting 75 miles an hour down that hill.

"Watch it, Gary!" came quietly from Dave, beside me.

"I can't! It's stuck!"

Panicking, I slammed on the brakes instead of turning off the ignition to kill the power, and at the bottom of the hill we skidded broadside into another car, knocking it winding. It was a miracle the other driver wasn't killed. Dave and Bill, in the car with me, were thrown under the dashboard, shaken up but not seriously hurt. I had a few scratches, hardly more than I'd have gotten in a good fight. But the Hudson was totaled — the crash completely wiped it out.

Then, irony of ironies, my stepfather — who was in one of his non-drinking periods at the time — happened to come along in a car with several of his fellow-workmen. They stopped, and he saw his pride and joy, the 1952 Hudson, wrecked and useless. He just shook his head, got back in the car and asked the men to drive on. He simply could not acknowledge to himself or others that such a thing could have happened to him. That night, he hit the bottle again, and it was a long time before he sobered up.

Soon afterwards I worked long enough to manage to get a motorcycle, and not long after that, I became part of a typical motorcycle gang.

Riding my Harley "chopper" was a double thrill, because most of the time I was at least half-loaded. There were seven of us in the gang, and we had a significant name — the "One Time." Whatever it was we were doing, we figured we'd wrap it all up in just one time. We'd get into drinking contests, to see who could polish off the most quarts of beer without stopping. Mostly, we rode on weekends, but it was a regular beat . . . we'd tear off in any direction, just looking for trouble.

We'd imagine ourselves to be like the movie stars in "The Wild One," and we'd "One Time" everyone and everything in sight. But there came a day in the summer of 1956 when the rest of the gang had gone elsewhere, so I picked up one of my good friends — a boy named Gary Hurt — and we managed to buy a couple of six-packs of beer (it was always easy to fake our age, or to get some drunken sailor to make the actual purchase for us). Then we headed for the mountains on my "bike." We first zoomed up the coast highway toward Malibu, then took off up one of the canyon roads, buzzing along and guzzling the beer, with Gary on behind me.

By the time we got to the top, we were pretty well loaded, and we had the idea we were mighty cool cats . . . we were acting real tough. We stopped at a bar, where we conned the guy into selling us some more beer, and when we came swaggering out, my motorcycle had fallen over.

When I picked it up, I knew we had trouble. "Look," I said, pointing at the problem, "gas-line is cracked."

"Sure is," he agreed. "Can't very well fix it here. What'll we do?"

I hesitated only a moment. "Ride 'er down!" I proclaimed. "Can't let a little thing like that stop us!"

It was leaking a steady drip of gasoline, but we were so well sloshed ourselves that off we went. I wanted to get down out of the mountains and have the gas-line fixed, so we started moving out fast. I turned up the throttle and let her rip.

We were hitting close to eighty, going around curves down

the mountain, with gas flying all over me from the leaking line. The bike was working fine despite the gas leak, and once down we'd have plenty of time to get it repaired. We almost flew down that mountain, and once we were back on the coast highway, we hightailed it some more until we got to Manhattan Beach. The further we went, the more soaked my pantlegs became with the leaking gasoline, but I didn't care. We had to slow down finally, because a motorcycle officer was ahead of us, and I came up beside him when he paused at a stoplight.

It was just after the officer took off in front of us that it happened. My bike blew up. The gasoline sparked from something, and there was a deafening explosion beneath us that sent Gary flying off the back while I went out over the handlebars. Soaked as I was, I became a human torch from the waist down, and I took off running and screaming. My whole right side was on fire, and I could only think of running from that awful burning.

I rolled in the dirt — rolled and rolled — but the fire kept on. So I got up and ran some more, shrieking with pain. Finally, Gary managed to catch up with me, and he jerked off what was left of my burning pants. Then he managed to roll me in the dirt some more, and snuff out the flames that were eating me alive.

The pain was indescribable, and as I lay there moaning, it seemed as if years went by before an ambulance finally came for me. It was like hellfire and damnation, and there were people gathered around staring at me like I was an animal in a circus. Newspaper photographers showed up and were busy snapping pictures like I was a sideshow freak. And all the time, the pain from my burns was setting me on fire again — and I couldn't keep from screaming.

When the ambulance men arrived, one of them jumped out with splints and started binding up my right leg.

"No, no!" I yelled. "It ain't broke — it's burned! I'm burnt all over! Get me to a hospital!"

The bike had blazed to a crisp and was just a bunch of twisted metal and rubber and stink when the fire department finally extinguished the flames. But I didn't care. All I wanted was to be rid of the excruciating torment knifing my body.

The ambulance drove from Manhattan Beach to Torrance and Harbor General Hospital, and it was an endless, murderous, agonizing ride. I thought I was dying and I only wished I would hurry up. It was the longest ride of my life.

When they wheeled me in on the stretcher, the agony was so intense I couldn't help screaming at the top of my lungs. They put me in the emergency ward, a large room with just some curtains separating its various units. And I still couldn't keep from hollering with pain.

Finally a nurse came in. "Why don't you shut up?" she snapped at me. "You're acting like a little baby."

She could have saved her breath. Perhaps she really didn't know what had happened to me; maybe she didn't care. I kept on yelling, and finally a doctor came and gave me a heavy shot of morphine. Within a short time, I was transported from the depths of hell to the heights of heaven. The pain left me, and the world was suddenly a totally different place.

"Thank you!" I said to the nurse. "Thank you. Thank you!" I suppose I was reacting not only to the morphine, but also the effects of the alcohol still in my system.

They kept me comfortable with morphine all that night, and the next day after dressing the burns carefully, they released me and told me to see my own doctor. I didn't need any urging, with all the pain I'd undergone, so I went to the doctor, and he gave me a prescription for codeine pills to hold down the pain. There were twenty-four pills in the bottle, and I hit that bottle hard. After two days, I'd used them all, and I went back for more.

For a while it looked like I'd have to have a skin graft on my heel, which had been badly seared. When I'd change the bandages on my burns, everyone else would leave the house, because the odor was so bad and the flesh-turned-green was enough to make a person throw up. But gradually the burns healed up, even if the treatment didn't. I kept on taking codeine pills for seven months, long after the pain from the burns was gone. It was the start of the pill scene, for me. I'd sniffed just about everything, and I'd tried alcohol in most of its forms, but up to that point, I hadn't gotten high on pills. The codeine hooked me without my knowing it. I became a walking zombie.

My folks finally realized I was getting strung out. "Gary, you've got to stop taking that codeine," my mother told me. "You're going to get hooked."

I laughed. "Who, me? No way!" I said. I was a bigshot, not one of those weaklings who'd let drugs get the best of him. No way.

But I kept taking codeine, because I had a bear by the tail and couldn't let go. Gradually I got back on joy water and amphetamines, whatever I could find . . . uppers, downers, the whole string.

From a normal weight of around 175, I dropped to 135 pounds. I couldn't sleep. I was unhappier than ever. But I kept drinking whatever I could get my hands on, and I kept taking whatever pills I could turn up. Although I never got on a motorcycle again, I hustled, lied, stole, and worked till I got hold of a used car and became part of a car club — the "Trojans."

It was a lot like the "One Time," except we spent our time dragging up and down Inglewood Boulevard and drinking lots of liquor. There were many times when I was stopped by the cops, and I spent a few overnight stretches in the pokey.

Once I sideswiped a guy's car and took off as fast as I could, because I didn't want any more accidents on my record, and I'd had enough to drink that I was scared they'd throw the book at me. I'd gone only a short distance when all of a sudden, it sounded like every siren in the County of Los Angeles was on my tail. Police cars swarmed over me from every direction. I was cornered. There was nothing to do but give up — and all because of a little old hit-and-run without too much damage. I was shocked . . . and scared!

They roughly shook me down, but I didn't have anything on me — no gun, no knife, not even the pills I was usually high on, because I'd taken them all.

"Hey, what's the gig?" I asked one of the policemen as they were fixing to haul me off to the station.

"You ought to know!" he sneered. "Armed robbery — what else?"

"Hey, you got the wrong guy!" I protested. "I ain't pulled no armed robbery!"

"No — you weren't down at the liquor store at Inglewood and El Segundo, were you?"

My mouth flew open. They *did* have the wrong guy! "You better believe I wasn't!" I yelled at him.

About that time, another officer came up and tapped the shoulder of the one who'd accused me. "What was the time on that robbery?" he asked.

The first one checked his notebook. "Ten-twenty," he said. "Why?"

"This dude's driving this Olds?" he asked.

"Right."

"Wasn't him, then," the second one said quietly. "I just got a radio report: this one clocked a hit-and-run down on Rosecrans near Crenshaw — ten-seventeen. Couldn't have got to . . ."

"You hit someone with your car tonight, buddy?"

They had me, cold turkey, but maybe it was a good thing, and I knew it. I nodded. "Just rubbed his car a little," I said. "Didn't do any damage."

The second officer shook his head. "Not the way I heard it," he said. "You scratched him pretty good. What'd you run for?"

"Scared!" I said. "I'm running scared most all the time."

"You mainlining?" he asked me then.

"Good Lord, no!" I protested. I'd never shot the big H, and I didn't want them thinking I had.

"We'll have to book you on the hit-run," he said. "But you couldn't have pulled the liquor store job. Come on."

It wasn't my first, nor my last, encounter with the law. And it wasn't the only time I was cleared by a circumstance of fate. But it gave me a taste of what it meant to be on the wrong side of the law.

Not long after that, the "Trojans" got in a gang war with the "Top Hats," and one night they caught one of our guys alone and hauled him out to stomp him. We saw them, but there were only five of us in my car, to twenty-five of them, and there wasn't anything we could do. Donny, our member, was so badly beaten our club was never the same. We decided to call it off so the black jackets with the gold horse's head on the back, our Trojan emblem, became something out of the past.

* * * *

It was around this time in 1958, that my stepfather and mother split for Seattle, Washington, leaving me on my own. Bud enlisted in the Air Force to get away from all the troubles at home, so I was by myself. I spent most of my time finding new ways to get loaded, always running away from the yawning chasm inside.

Occasionally some of us would go into a drugstore and buy nose inhalers and break them open and get the cotton out and cut it into four separate pieces. Then we'd put the cotton in our mouths and drink cola to force it down. The next thing we knew, we'd be riding high (or so we thought).

The worst of it was, when we came down off one of those highs, we'd be so nervous we couldn't handle it, and we'd have to take it again, to go right back up. Trying to get off that particular combination of drugs was disaster — we had to take something else, or we'd flip out. There was no way to fill the emptiness, so we'd keep right on with the drugs — anything we could get to blow our minds.

I slept in the car and existed on shark meat I picked out of the garbage cans at the fish markets at the pier. I also took on whatever liquid fire I could get my hands on. It was a wonder I managed to survive at all.

I kept on running. I even ran to Seattle, where my folks had moved. Since I'd traded my car for booze, I hitchhiked there, leaving behind me a trail of shame. Once there, though, I found little to aid me. My mother, thinking it would help, took me to Alcoholics Anonymous. But I could feel the taste of drugs in my mouth, and I couldn't wait to get away from the AA meeting.

When we went back home one evening my stepfather was waiting for us. "Take your choice!" he told her. "Either he goes or I do." And then he turned to me, "Get out! I'm not going to have you around here again to tear up everything we've finally managed to build! Out!"

I couldn't blame him. He was right; whatever they had built, I'd tear it down.

So I walked out, and within an hour I was back on the road to Los Angeles. I didn't have anything to go back to, but I didn't have anything to stay there for, either. Before I left, my mother managed to slip a twenty-dollar bill into my hand. And by the time I'd caught a ride down the California-bound highway, I was already well-loaded. I was back in my own dream world, running from reality, and going downhill all the way.

Chapter Five

The road from Seattle to Los Angeles is a long and dreary one when you're bumming from town to town like I was. By now, I was so used to abusing my body with alcohol, pills, and neglect I was nothing more than a third-class tramp, a hobo. I'd eat and drink whatever I could find; usually someone else's leftovers. I'd cadge a buck any way I could, even if I had to work a little. It was a miserable existence.

Sleeping in culverts or any other place I could find, I finally managed to get back to Redondo Beach, where I met a guy called Pidge. He was a white freak. He stayed high most of the time on "whites," a type of amphetamine pill. I soon joined him and turned into a white freak myself.

How long this existence went on, I am not sure. It was one long, crazy time. I slept in the back of an old car, often going days at a time without a square meal. But if I could get high on pills or alcohol or a combination of both, I didn't care. I just wanted to run and run and run from reality.

It wasn't always on booze or pills, either. One time, without intending to, I found out what gasoline can do to you. I was in Pidge's garage syphoning some gas from his tank to put in a car I'd borrowed, and I accidentally swallowed a mouthful of it.

Talk about the explosive power of gasoline — that stuff took me right off the ground! It almost blew my head off my shoulders. I felt like I'd been tossed up in the air by a bomb, and I started jumping around that garage like an Indian doing his war dance.

Pidge thought I'd really flipped, and the way I was floating, I wasn't so sure I hadn't. But I knew for sure I didn't want any more gasoline highs — that one time was more than enough of that. I'd sniffed gasoline at The Hacienda and gotten an idea of what it would do, but drinking it was something else. I'm convinced that any bigger dose would have been lethal. But within hours after that, I'd taken on enough liquor and pills to forget about ever having tasted gasoline.

Despite the fact I could never get along with my family — especially my stepfather — I was lonely without them, and once again I took to the road, landing in Seattle. I found as long as I didn't try to stay in their home, we could get along fine. My stepfather would tolerate me, just so I wasn't underfoot all the time. And I could pick up some easy money from my mother, if I didn't come around with my hand out too often.

It was easy to make friends because I wasn't alone in my run from reality. There was a boy there named John, about my age, and he introduced me to some cough medicine called Robitussin. A couple of ounces of it, along with a couple of beers, and I'd be loaded for eight hours straight.

John and I got a room in an old hotel, down in the basement, and we'd freak out real often with Robitussin and beer. Then we'd just lie there in that room, and do all sorts of goofed-up things. Once I took John's .45 pistol and shot holes in the wall, and then we had a giggling, laughing fit about it, thinking that was really the sharpest thing anyone could possibly do.

Along with the gun, John had a bolo knife, and we'd practice throwing that knife at the wall, so we'd know what to do in case we ran into somebody and had to use it as a weapon in a fight. What a trip! We thought we were really cool.

At night, we'd drive around town picking up girls which was easy to do, because there were plenty of them running from themselves the same way we were. There was one girl, Janie, whom I liked, and one night the three of us decided to go to a party. When we got there, we found it was just a bunch of fellows, and that they'd already exhausted their supplies of booze.

"Hey, let's go get some more wine!" one of them said.

So without even thinking, John and I left Janie at the party and took off. We cruised around a while, and finally got around to picking up the wine we wanted, but we didn't feel like waiting to join the others at the party to sample it, so there wasn't really any rush about returning.

When we did get back, the place was almost deserted. There was just one guy left, and he was on a high of his own.

"Where'd everybody go? Where's Janie?" I asked him.

He just pointed in the direction of the bedroom, not saying a word, so I headed in there in a hurry. Janie was lying on the bed, face down, crying.

"Hey, what happened?" I asked.

She kept her head down, so I could hardly make out the words. "When you left," she said in a muffled voice, "they — they grabbed me and — raped me." Her sobs shook her body, and all I could think about was catching those rats and teaching them a lesson they'd never forget. I rushed out to get John.

"Come on!" I yelled. "Let's go get your forty-five!"

On the way to the hotel, I told him what had happened, and he picked up both the gun and the knife when we got to our room. Then we went back, but by then, Janie was gone, and only the freaked-out guy was still there. He didn't know where the others were.

So we spent the next several hours looking in the neighborhood bars and along the streets, but we never did catch sight of the attackers. John was getting madder by the minute, and knowing his temper, I wasn't sure what he'd do.

"Maybe they made for the beach," I suggested, and John wheeled around and headed toward a beach area we sometimes frequented. But it was empty and John took his forty-five and began shooting it out over the water.

It wasn't long until a police car showed up. "What's going on?" was the quick question.

I'd grabbed the gun and hid it in the car only moments before they arrived. I told the cop what happened to Janie and how we thought the guys who raped her might be at the beach. Apparently, the story made sense, because the cop went to his car with no more questions.

"Let us know if you find them," he said before driving off. "We'll take it from there."

"Sure," I said, and John and I went back to the territory where the party had been held. But we didn't find the gang, nor did I ever see Janie again. All of them just disappeared from sight.

* * * *

It was shortly after this, during the summer of 1960, that our family fortunes changed. My stepfather unexpectedly inherited close to $75,000 when his father died. And suddenly I was welcome in my mother's and stepfather's home once more. I was more than a little surprised, for I'd given him more than enough reason never to open his door to me again. But I did avoid staying with them, preferring to remain on my own. There had been too many run-ins and incidents in the past.

And now in finding a welcome I hadn't experienced in previous years, I didn't question it; I just took advantage of it. I figured the world owed me a living. My folks bought a fine home, a 38-foot cabin cruiser, all the comforts of wealth, and I had them, too.

The first thing my stepfather did was to pay off what was owed on the car my brother, Bud, had left in my care. It was to have been my responsibility to make the payments on it but now I had a beautiful 1952 Oldsmobile to drive free and clear. I'd also have $50 to $100 a day handed to me — whatever I asked. And my stepfather would load the trunk of the car with a case of beer though I hadn't quite turned 21, knowing if I didn't get it from him, I'd get it some other way. He was once again, as he had in earlier times when I was a Boy Scout, trying to be a good father, but he was only feeding my habit.

It took me a long time to learn that all the wonderful friends I had were buddies only because I had a car and money and booze. Take these all away, and they'd be gone so fast there'd be only a cloud of dust left behind.

But finally the realization of what my life had become began to catch up with me. For one thing, Robitussin — the mainstay of my drug habit — was suddenly taken off the open market and

placed on prescription, because it contained an opium deriva-
tive. That meant I couldn't buy it as easily, and I panicked,
because I was hooked on the stuff.

Then one of my buddies told me about terpin hydrate and
codeine — an elixir or cough syrup that was easily available. So I
bought a bottle and drank it, and it was horrible-tasting! My
buddy had told me to suck a lemon to get the stuff down, and I
could sure see why. But I made the switch from Robitussin to
terpin hydrate and I began drinking the stuff every day. It was
an easy way to stay loaded, and that's the way I wanted to stay.

There were a few times, however, when I'd face up to my
problems for brief periods, and in those intervals, my mother
and stepfather did their best to help me. They urged me to
return to Alcoholics Anonymous. But my problem was drugs,
not alcohol, and I couldn't see much help from that source.

They suggested doctors, a sanitarium where I could break
my habit, other solutions, but I wasn't ready for them. Finally
my mom came up with a new one: "Bud did real good when he
joined the Air Force," she said. "Maybe you'd find it easier to
get straightened out if you joined the service, Gary."

At first I was inclined to reject this idea just as I had all the
others, but I really was searching for an answer to my problems,
and this one seemed as logical as anything else I'd heard. I knew
there'd be strict discipline in whatever branch of service I might
enter, and deep down, I knew that's what I really needed.

But I had to drag my feet. It was a matter of principle with
me, always to rebel at anything anyone else suggested. "I'm too
strung out, Mom," I said. "They'd never let me enlist."

But she'd already done some checking. "You're registered
for the draft," she said. "All you have to do is volunteer for the
draft, and you'll be in the Army — and maybe a whole lot better
off."

It didn't take long, and before I knew it, I was taking all kinds
of Army tests, to see if I had any skills that were usable in the
service. I didn't. They decided to make me a walking soldier,
and I went into basic training for the infantry at Fort Ord,
California, in January, 1961.

What followed were four of the worst weeks in my life. Being new to the Army, I was just a scared recruit, along with a lot of others, and I was forced to kick my drug habit out of sheer necessity. It was miserable! I had constant diarrhea. My stomach cramped with piercing pain. It was so bad I'd run down to the beach, to get away from everyone else. I didn't dare admit I had been on drugs. And finally, after the first four weeks, my body adjusted, and I once again felt like a human being.

Things went well for a time. I was sent back to Fort Lewis, Washington, and assigned to drive a jeep and equipped with a 106 recoilless rifle, and I enjoyed that. I also drove a two-and-a-half ton truck to haul other soldiers around. There were always three square meals a day, and I was over the pangs of withdrawal. Life was good.

But like all the other good times before that, I just couldn't stand things going better and better. We were scheduled to go out on bivouac, and whether I was scared of that forthcoming new experience or just the old habits asserting themselves, I will never know, but whatever it was, I went into town ahead of time and got myself a pint of whiskey, then went to the drugstore and bought some asthmador — a grayish powder someone had told me would get me high quick — and a bunch of empty capsules. That night, I made up about two hundred asthmador pills, and the next day, I drove one of the trucks out into the mountains where we were to have our three-day bivouac.

Like the others, I set up my pup-tent, and managed to keep my whiskey and pills well-hidden from anyone else. I even went to bed at the same time as the rest, but somewhere in the back of my mind was that compulsion to get loaded. I didn't want to get too high, because I knew if I did, I'd get caught. So I only took about ten of the pills and half the whiskey. Somewhere, I'd misfigured.

I have no memory of what happened, but I remember what I was told about myself. It was four in the morning, and from out of the pre-dawn darkness came a wild scream that woke everyone in the area. Through sleepy eyes, they saw an incredible sight — a tent gyrating around and then galloping off down into the nearby trees.

Our Company B lieutenant was quick to the occasion: "Go

down there and catch that tent and tie it up with rope!'' he roared. ''Whatever it is inside there, bring it up and put it in my jeep!''

The next thing I knew, I was being bounced along in the back of the jeep, half-suffocated from being tied up in my tent. It was wretchedly hot, but I was shaking all over with cold chills, and I could hardly breathe. The deadly combination I'd taken was giving me convulsions.

Finally, we got back to the base, the tent was unwrapped, and I was unceremoniously marched in to face my company captain.

''Soldier,'' he snapped, ''what's wrong with you?''

''Nothing.''

''Nothing, what?''

''Nothing, *sir!*''

The captain stared at me for a moment, then nodded to the other soldiers beside me. ''Search him!'' he said, and they pushed me up against the orderly room wall and shook me down. The pills were the first thing they found, hidden in every pocket of my clothes.

The captain looked at the handful of capsules, opened one, and sniffed it. Then he looked soberly at me. ''You're in trouble, soldier,'' he said. ''Don't you know you could go to federal prison for possession of illegal drugs?''

I hung my head. ''Yes, sir,'' I said quietly. I figured it was no use telling him the asthmador powder wasn't an illegal narcotic. I knew I was on the way to the stockade, for sure. I'd blown it again!

But I got a padded cell instead, part of the mental ward in the base hospital. It was the first time I'd been in a place like that, and it was frightening. I didn't know what to expect.

I wasn't tied down, or anything like that, but I was in a type of solitary confinement. And there was a constant stream of doctors, looking through a little window at me. I felt like a monkey in a zoo. Occasionally the doctors would lead me out and sit me down and act like I was a little kid. They'd ask me questions about drugs. What had I taken the asthmador for? Why did I take drugs in the first place? One would ask questions a while, and then someone else would come along, and he'd ask the same questions all over again.

"Do you like the service, Private Fisher?"

I shrugged my shoulders. "It's okay."

"Do you feel you need psychiatric help?"

"Naw, I just need to get out of here and back to my company. I'll be all right."

"You'd just go back to taking drugs though, wouldn't you, Private Fisher?"

I shook my head. "Naw, I don't want any more of that," I said. "That was a real bad trip."

"You've been on trips like that before?"

I didn't want to stick my neck out, but I was afraid to lie to them, because I didn't know what would happen. "Not like that one!"

I didn't get back to my company — not until I'd spent a lot of time there. I'd gone AWOL from The Hacienda, and I thought about leaving Fort Lewis the same way, after they let me out of the padded cell and had me staying in a regular hospital ward.

But when I wandered out onto the patio, I saw the walls were sixteen to eighteen feet high, and I knew there was no way out of there except whatever way the Army officials arrived at. It was several weeks before I finally got the word: court martial! It was no fun facing the panel of sober-faced officers. I went through a lot of the same questions I'd answered for the doctors, but I kept repeating I only wanted to get back to my company, and I'd be all right. I was quite surprised when they sent me back to B Company — I'd had visions of ending up in an Army prison somewhere.

After that I didn't use drugs for quite a spell, and things began to look up again. But once more I couldn't stand the good life. So I began buying terpin hydrate cough medicine and getting quietly high every night. And for quite some time I got by with it. There were no more of those wild incidents like I'd pulled on bivouac, and I managed to stumble through my days until I could get my dose of medicine at night. Most of the time, I and a black soldier, who'd turned his rifle on an officer, were assigned to digging latrine ditches and then filling them up.

Needless to say, it wasn't a very inspiring existence.

Then came an unexpected inspection, one of those surprise affairs they sometimes call a "shakedown." There wasn't time to get ready for it, and when the inspecting officers opened my footlocker, the handwriting on the wall showed up in the stack of terpin hydrate bottles I'd hidden in it.

This time, the Army didn't fool around. I went before another court martial in a matter of days, and almost immediately afterward, I was called before the colonel who was base commander, and told I was to be discharged from the service.

"You're going out on a Section 208," he told me sternly. "Do you know what that means, soldier?"

I had a good idea, but I wasn't sure. "No, sir," I said.

"That means you're leaving the service on a medical discharge," the colonel said, looking me in the eye. "But it's not a disability discharge. It's an 'unfit for military service' medical discharge." I turned my eyes away from his steady gaze. "I think you know why."

I knew why, all right; there was no room for drug addicts in Uncle Sam's Army. Back then, the drug problems with soldiers in Vietnam and other foreign areas hadn't come along yet.

"Good luck, Mister." I was not a soldier any longer. I took the discharge paper, dated December 22, 1961, and they sent me to the supply room where they gave me a silly looking brown suit. But they let me keep my combat boots, and I must have been a ridiculous sight with the odd-ball clothes and those boots.

It didn't matter. I headed for downtown Seattle, only a hop, skip and jump from Fort Lewis. That same night I found a pre-Christmas party and got loaded on drugs once more. Gary Fisher — the drug derelict who'd gone into the Army to try to get squared around — had struck out again. There was nothing to do but keep on running and keep from facing who I was, and that meant getting plastered on whatever I could get my hands on.

Chapter Six

When you lose your self-respect, you're pretty far gone. No matter what others think of you, as long as you can retain at least a few shreds of self-respect, you can go on believing there's hope. "If only. . ." and there's always a ready list of things and people to blame. But those shreds were getting mighty thin in my life.

My mother and stepfather were really disgusted when the Army booted me out. I think they'd relied on the United States military service to come through where they'd failed, and when it didn't happen, they were bitter. So there was nothing for me in Seattle, and I took to the road again — frustrated, unhappy, saddled with a drug habit I couldn't control, not caring if I lived or died.

As usual, I made no preparations for the journey. I simply decided on impulse to head south. Maybe the weather was partially responsible, for it was snowing in Seattle and it was a biting cold that cut through to the bone. I remembered pleasant days on the beach in southern California, forgetting, of course, all the unpleasant times I'd had there, as well.

So up went the thumb. I would hitchhike to Los Angeles, as I'd done so many times in the past, and the grass would be greener on that other side of the fence. I stood on the side of the highway for what seemed hours, and the longer I stood and watched the cars whiz by, the sorrier I felt for myself. Life simply wasn't worth living any longer. Why fight a losing battle?

Traffic had thinned by this time, for it was early morning,

and it didn't take any great act of courage to lie down in the middle of the road. At least, I didn't have to undergo the exhaustion of standing in the raw cold anymore — I could rest my weary body on the icy, snow-covered pavement, and who cared what happened after that?

From where I lay, I could see far up the highway, and out of the gloom came bright headlights with small amber lights above them — obviously, a big truck.

This is it, I thought. I wonder if that driver will see me? And if he does see me, will he be able to halt that rig with all the ice on this road? Oh, well, who cares?

So I lay and watched that monster descend on me, and I suppose I must have felt some relief when I heard the hiss of the air brakes as the driver rolled to a standstill only inches from my shivering body. He didn't waste any time jumping down from his cab.

"What in hell is wrong with you fellah?" he yelled as he stood over me. "Are you crazy?"

I didn't really want to answer that question. "I'm — sick!" I managed to squeeze out. "Awful sick!"

"Well, you sure picked one helluva way to get better!" the driver said, reaching down to grab my arm. "Come on — I'm taking you to a doctor!"

I let him pull me to my feet and boost me up into the cab of the big truck. I didn't say thanks because I wasn't sure whether I appreciated what he'd done. I wasn't sure at all I wanted to keep on going. So I just sat there, noticing that every once in a while, the driver would glance over at me and shake his head. I think he was more anxious to get rid of me than any load he ever hauled.

By the time we rolled into the next town down the road, I'd decided maybe I could make it. It wasn't snowing, and it was warm in the truck cab, and if I could find a bottle of terpin hydrate, I could get loaded, and things wouldn't look so bad.

"You can just let me out anywhere here," I said to my benefactor.

He looked relieved. "Sure you don't want me to find a doctor for you?" he asked.

"No, I'll be okay," I said. Then, trying to make it sound

convincing, "I got some friends here who'll take care of me."

I could tell he wasn't taken in by that story. "Okay," he said. "Just don't try that stunt you pulled on me, again. The next guy might not see you in time."

"No way!" I said to him. "I'm — glad you stopped."

He began to slow the truck. "You need money?" he asked then.

I'd never been bashful about accepting a handout, whenever and from whomever I could get it. "Well, I —" I hung my head. It was an act I'd practiced, successfully, on many previous occasions.

"Here's a five-spot," he said, holding out a bill. "Sorry, that's all I got."

"Gee, thanks, buddy!" I managed a weak smile. "I sure appreciate that!"

The rig stopped, and I opened the door of the cab and jumped down, still hearing the hiss of those marvelous air brakes that had kept the mammoth on wheels from crushing the life out of me. Deep down, I was grateful. I'd decided, during that brief ride, that I wasn't really ready to cash it all in — not yet. I needed just one more high, and now I could get on it.

The big truck roared away, and I began to look around. I probably wouldn't find an all-night drugstore open, I knew, but it didn't matter. I'd already stuck my hand in my pocket to keep it warm, and found the reassuring shape of a terpin hydrate bottle there. I remembered that I'd managed to buy an extra bottle before I took to the road. It was right there all the time, deep in my pocket. All I needed was some place to sack out.

I knew what to look for — a cheap hotel that didn't have any bathrooms in the rooms themselves . . . just publicly-shared bathrooms at the end of the halls. It was easy for me to walk in like I belonged, climb the stairs, and lock myself in one of those lavatories. I'd done it before, and after walking a while, I found just what I was looking for. There, in that cramped little smelly room, I choked down the terpin hydrate, then crawled into the confines of the narrow bathtub to spend the rest of the night. It wasn't restful; people were constantly knocking on the door, wanting in, but I didn't care. I was loaded, and that was all that mattered. By morning, I was stiff and sore, but still high, and I crippled out of my forlorn roost, anxious to get on my way.

It was easier to thumb a ride in the daytime, even though I was a scroungy-looking sight. There was always someone who'd take pity and stop to pick me up. I'd learned in my many treks back and forth that I could expect anything, often a homosexual proposition. Those I'd learned to play along, to get as far down the road as I could, and then turn them off, perhaps leaving a sadder but wiser deviate behind me.

It was easy enough to make the old connections when I got back to the Los Angeles area, and within a short time, I'd established myself again in Redondo Beach. I managed to get a job in a service station, and with the money I earned, I was able to get a room in a cheap hotel. I could somehow make it through the days and get good and loaded at night. But now there was a difference: I had a reputation.

I was in my hotel room one night, when there came a knock on the door. I opened it to see two uniformed men standing there. "You Gary Fisher?" one of them asked.

I wondered how they knew who I was. "That's my name," I said, trying to sound nonchalant.

"Police officers," the other officer said. "We'd like to ask you some questions."

I hadn't done anything I knew of, except get loaded on liquor and drugs. "Sure," I said. "Come on in."

They looked around the room, but I'd learned long ago to keep my terpin hydrate bottles or any other evidence of my habit hidden away from prying eyes.

"Like to know where you were last night, Gary," the first cop said. "About this time of evening."

I thought a minute. I'd gotten loaded early the night before, but I was pretty sure I hadn't gone out. "I was right here in my room," I told them.

They both nodded. "Like to have you take a little ride with us," one of them said. "Okay?"

I still didn't know what was coming off. "Sure," I said, wishing I'd at least gotten a few pills down before they came along. I didn't feel the best inside, but maybe I could stand it, whatever they had in mind.

We closed my room, walked down the one flight of stairs and got in their black and white automobile. The officers continued to be courteous and friendly. There was no indication I was under arrest, or for that matter, under suspicion. We were just going for a pleasant little evening drive.

The drive turned out to be a fairly short one, to the nearby city of Torrance. Once there, we drove into a residential section, finally stopping in front of a big corner apartment house with a large picture window in front. There was a bright street light, and one of the cops took my arm and stood me in front of the car, under that light.

"Would you please stand right here for a while, Gary?" he asked politely.

It didn't make any sense, but I was agreeable. No point in hassling it. "Okay," I said.

The second policeman went into the apartment house, then, after I'd stood there a while, he came out, shaking his head at the second cop. "Guess we've made a mistake," he said. "Sorry about that." And he motioned for me to get back into the car.

We drove back to my hotel room, and on the way, the officers explained there'd been a burglary, and I'd been picked out of a group of line-up photos as a possible suspect. But upon seeing me in person, the witness to the burglary had been sure I wasn't the one, after all. So I went back to my lonely room, and wasted no time in getting well-loaded for the night . . . the unnerving experience of being hauled around in a cop-car made me want to forget everything in a hurry. The next day, I moved to a nearby motel room, hoping to lose the fuzz in case they had any more ideas concerning me.

About a week later, there was another loud knock on the door of my room. I hesitated. I didn't want to go through that routine again, and I was quite certain none of my friends would be coming to the motel room, at least not that early in the evening. So I didn't move thinking maybe whoever it was would go away. I just lay quietly on my bed.

Abruptly, the door crashed open, and two men — one with a gun in his hand — charged into my room. Before I could move, they grabbed my arm and pulled me off the bed, then slammed me face-first against the wall.

"Put your hands up on the wall! Spread your legs!" they snapped.

While one held the gun on me, the other searched me thoroughly, top to bottom. Only then did they identify themselves.

"FBI," one said. "Let me have your hands, please!"

I dropped my hands behind me, and could feel the cold steel of handcuffs being locked on.

"You have a right to remain silent if you wish," the second man said. "It's my duty to tell you that anything you say may be used against you. Come with us, please."

I didn't like the idea of a re-run. I'd been through this just the week before though in a lot milder fashion. So as we headed out the broken door, I asked the all-important question. "What's the charge?" I demanded.

The sober-faced FBI agent didn't answer immediately. He just kept walking, letting me wonder. Then he turned to face me, staring directly into my eyes.

"Murder," he said grimly.

My stomach flip-flopped. I'd never killed anyone; I'd never really tried to hurt anyone aside from an occasional fight, although I'd thought about it many times in my life.

"Hey, wait a minute!" I protested. "You got the wrong guy!"

We'd reached the car by now — an ordinary sedan — and one man slid behind the wheel, while the other got in back with me.

The one with me reached up and tapped the other on the shoulder. "Hey, George," he said. "Maybe, before we leave, we'd better check his hands."

"Right," the driver agreed, and he reached in his pocket for the key to the handcuffs they'd put on me, handing it to his partner.

With one cuff unshackled, the agent beside me said, "Let's see your hands, please."

I wondered what they could possibly want to look at my

hands for? But whatever it was, I wasn't about to argue with them. They'd made it plain they wouldn't stand for any nonsense. So I held out my hands.

"Palms up, please."

I did as I was told. First, they both looked carefully at my hands, in the dim glow from the domelight. Then they rubbed their own fingers over my hands, both men checking first my left, then my right hand.

"Not there!' the one called George exclaimed, shaking his head. "What do you know?"

The second man, the one beside me, grinned. "Well, you win a few, lose a few." Then, turning to me, "Lucky thing for you, you didn't have callouses on your hands."

I couldn't believe it. "You mean —"

"We know for a fact our guy had heavy callouses on his hands," he said, unlocking the remaining handcuff from my wrist. "You're free to go!"

I went, grateful for whatever providence had spared me from facing a murder charge. And the next morning, the motel proprietor — taking an understandably dim view of having some law officers knock down the door to my room — gave me the parting word.

So I got out, and later that day I was able to find a little house with a landlady who, I could tell from experience, was a wino, an alcoholic.

* * * *

My job petered out not long after, but I didn't care. I was tired of being told what to do and I was content to stay loaded day and night. I didn't care I was abusing my body and my mind beyond all reason. I didn't care about anything. I didn't know when to quit. There was one afternoon I was so totally loaded it was a wonder I hadn't passed out. I was walking back to the shack and passed a karate studio, a place where instructors taught people how to protect themselves with karate. For some reason I decided it was time to teach those karate experts a thing or two.

So I went inside, looking for a guy wearing a black belt which denoted the true karate craftsman. When I found him, "Like to fight you," I announced. "I had guerilla warfare training in the Army. How about it?"

The black belt wearer was friendly but firm. "Afraid not," he said. "We're not allowed to use our training that way."

I was just high enough to be stupidly stubborn. "Aw, come on!" I urged. "You can't hurt me. I'm an expert."

"Sorry. Can't do it."

I got sarcastic. "Scared, huh?" I goaded him. "I never did figure you karate cats amounted to very much. I'd probably take you apart, anyway."

Still smiling, he agreed. "Probably," he said.

Now I was getting mad. "All right," I grumbled, "are you going to take me on or not? Let's get it on!"

Apparently, he realized I wouldn't be satisfied until we'd had a go at it. "One condition," he said. "I'll have to ask you to sign a release stating I'm free of all responsibility for whatever happens to you. Okay?"

"Sure," I bragged. "Bring it on, I'll sign anything!"

He rummaged through his desk, and finally found a paper with some printing on it that I didn't bother to try to read, knowing I wouldn't get beyond the first three-syllable word, anyway. "This means you can't sue me or my employer if you're hurt," he said. "You understand that?"

I laughed. "Me get hurt? You gotta be kidding!" I scratched my signature on the paper, a slow process since I'd never really learned to write, and I always had trouble even getting my name signed.

"This way, please." My karate expert partner was over-polite as he pointed to the mat where we would go at it. I had visions of really giving this guy a lesson on how to fight, dating back to my childhood experience, the practice in kicking I'd had at The Hacienda, and the brief army training in finding vulnerable spots. I figured I could lay him out cold.

But the visions were only that — a fleeting imaginary glimpse of what might have happened, for once on the mat, I never knew what hit me. I didn't land a single blow. That karate master was all around me and all over me. I was sure he'd broken both my arms, my legs, and my back. When he stopped, I couldn't move. He'd simply paralyzed me, top to bottom. I could only sit there and stare dumbly at him.

"Satisfied?" He grinned at me.

I grunted, struggling to my feet. Every bone in my body protested, and I didn't feel as high as I had when I walked in.

"That's enough," I said. "No more." And I dragged myself outside. I was the guy who was always going to pull off a big one, and always fell flat on my face. I managed to get back to my abode, and later that day, when the landlady gave me some money to buy her a couple of fifths of vodka, I took the loot and bought myself some "speed" pills instead, to put the stinging memory of the afternoon's fiasco behind me. I never went back to the shack.

It wasn't long though before I found a trailer to stay in — a spot where I could continue to spend my days and nights in my favorite pastime. Not long after, while riding a high, I fell from the pier at Redondo one day, and fractured my right leg. I ended up with a cast from ankle to thigh, and this turned into a mixed blessing for me, for I could get lots of sympathy and some cold cash with that leg in a cast.

I was getting to be a real con artist in playing on people's pity. There was one poor soul who owned a fried chicken eatery, and I really got him going. For a time, he'd bring me a bucket of chicken and a five-dollar-bill every evening. I think he was really just trying to be a Good Samaritan, but his efforts were a bit misguided where I was concerned. I'd eat some of the chicken, give the rest away, and then take the five bucks and trade it for whatever I needed to get loaded again.

But it was too good to last, and my benefactor finally decided there were better things to do with his surplus. So I had to hustle cash any other way I could. One time, I got so desperate I sold my best friend to a cocktail waitress — for ten dollars, so I could grab some drugs. My best friend, in this case, was a Siamese cat which I'd stolen. That cat was one of the most understanding creatures I'd ever known, never asking more than I could deliver, never pressuring me for anything . . . she had really turned me on. After I'd sold that beautiful animal with the brown silk coat and cobalt blue eyes, I got high on wine and had an hour-long crying jag thinking about how much I'd miss her.

The wine spree lasted quite a while. I just lay on my bed in the little trailer, staring at the ceiling and sweating and wondering what I could do for a lift. Suddenly I was surprised to see a large lizard crawling on the ceiling above me. I watched him awhile and thought back to my days as a kid when I used to catch lizards around the house my folks had in Redondo. I'd take a hot soldering iron and ram it down their throats, just for kicks. I wondered how this big lizard would like that kind of go-round.

Then, suddenly, there was not just one lizard, but five of them — big ones. They were all over that ceiling. Without warning, one of them dropped on my chest. I let out a scream as I tried to scrape him off, but I couldn't get rid of him. Then the others dropped on me, and I could see lizards all over that trailer. They'd come back to get even for the times I jammed the sizzling soldering iron down their throats — I knew it!

Hearing my screams, a girl in the house in front of the trailer, who'd helped me before, came running back to the trailer. "What is it, Gary? What's wrong?"

"Lizards!" I shrieked. "They're all over me! Get 'em off!"

Apparently Jeanie realized what the problem was, for she immediately began slapping at the lizards that were crawling all over me. It didn't help much, because the whole trailer was filled with large lizards by now, but Jeanie stayed and did battle with them, and one by one they disappeared. When they were gone, I was wet with cold sweat; my entire body was trembling; my breath came in labored spurts; I was totally exhausted.

"Get me something to drink, Jeanie!" I pleaded. "Quick!"

"Sure, Gary," she said. "Sure!" And she left me alone to recall the ghastly fear that had gripped me with all those grisly reptiles crawling over and under and all around me.

After I'd downed a shot of vodka, I began to face the reality of what had happened. I'd heard of the DT's, but I'd never imagined I'd experience them. It was frightening, perhaps more scary than anything I'd ever gone through. And I made up my mind right then I'd do something about it. I couldn't stand any more of that. There had to be a way to get this off my back.

I told Jeanie what I intended to do. "Oh, thank God, Gary!" she said. "I've been praying you'd see the light!" She was a religious girl, sincere in her beliefs, and anxious to help anyone she could. We took off the next morning for downtown Los Angeles, going directly to the County Hospital. It was a familiar area, not far from where I'd spent a lot of my childhood days at the boys' home.

With Jeanie beside me, it was a real effort to tell the receptionist at the hospital that I wanted to commit myself to the mental ward because of drug and alcohol addiction.

The girl at the desk looked at me like she couldn't believe me. "Sit down over there," she said, pointing to a waiting room.

Jeanie sat down with me, but I hadn't been there five minutes until I decided this was a mistake after all. "Come on!" I said. "Let's get out of here!"

She did her best to detain me. "Gary!" she pleaded. But it was no use. That hospital suddenly looked like a prison.

I got up and walked out, and she slowly followed. Outside, it didn't seem so bad. We walked around quite a while, and Jeanie reminded me of what happened the day before, and how I had to do something about my problems or I'd cash it all in.

"You wanted to come down here this morning," Jeanie refreshed my memory. "Isn't it about time you followed through on something worthwhile?"

"What's worthwhile about an old hospital?" I asked. "They're worse trouble than what I went through yesterday."

Jeanie turned my face with her hand, so I had to look her in the eyes. "You really don't mean that," she said.

The sight of those giant lizards flashed through my mind. "Okay," I said reluctantly. "Let's go back."

No sooner had I stepped inside the door when six men in uniform swarmed over me. Apparently the receptionist had sent out the word there was a live one running around the place. They stuffed me, not gently, into a strait jacket, while I struggled furiously to get away from them. I hadn't bargained for this. But it was no use. I was no match for six big men, and without even getting a chance to say goodbye to Jeanie, I was hustled off to a padded cell.

If I'd been looking for a different atmosphere than I'd been used to, I surely found it now. The room was even smaller than the one I'd hated at Fort Ord, when I went off the deep end on bivouac. Not only that, I was strapped tight to a bed. I couldn't move a muscle if I wanted to.

It was the beginning of the most terrifying time I'd ever experienced.

Chapter Seven

For a time after the door to the padded cell slammed shut, I wrestled with the bonds that held me to the bed, but it was no use. I simply could not move. How I wished I hadn't let Jeanie talk me into coming back that second time! What I wouldn't give for a drink . . . some pills . . . anything, even death.

But there was time to think, to wonder how I'd arrived at this sorry state, strapped down like a lunatic. Was I insane? The lizards of yesterday flicked across my mind.

I thought back over the years, sketches of my past flashing before my eyes. The first time I got drunk on booze . . . the first time I got high on pills . . . sniffing glue, paint thinner and gasoline . . . taking Robitussin . . . switching to terpin hydrate and codeine . . . how had it all happened? And now this!

I'd never get hooked, I had thought. No way! But here I was, tied to a bed in a padded cell, tied with a chain I'd forged myself: the first link, not heavy, not amounting to much, no problem; the second and third links, it's just a small chain, easily broken. But you keep adding links, and all of a sudden, it's big enough to wrap you up and chain you down and hold you fast, so you're not able to get loose. It happens so easily you're unaware of it until it's too late!

This was no hospital bed I was lying on. It was flat and hard, and there was no way for me to signal for an attendant, except to yell. I needed help now, so I yelled.

No one came, so I kept on yelling. It had been quite a time since I'd had any terpin hydrate — I'd been loaded on wine the day before — and as usual, with withdrawal came diarrhea. I needed miserably to immediately go to the bathroom and finally my yells brought a sour-faced nurse.

"What's your problem?"

"I need to go to the bathroom!" I said in desperation.

She glanced at her watch. "You can wait a while," she said casually.

"No, I can't!" I insisted. "I've got dia —"

"Oh, shut up!" she interrupted. "Stop sniveling!" And she walked out.

Not long after she'd gone, there was no way I could keep control any longer. I knew it was no use to yell again — she'd made that quite plain — so I gave up. Lying there in my own waste, I began to cry. And I couldn't even wipe away the tears.

How much later the same sour-faced nurse came to my cell, I do not know, but when she did, and discovered what had happened, I was subjected to a barrage of insulting language. She had to change the bedding, then clean me up — a messy job, to say the least. She was careful though to keep me strapped down the whole time.

Then, when she left, she laid a tray of food on my chest, but she loosened one wrist strap only enough so I could almost — but not quite — get the food to my mouth. Otherwise, I was still totally strapped down. So I yelled again. And yelled. And yelled.

Perhaps five minutes went by before the nurse stuck her head in the door of the cell. "What'd you do — dirty your pants again?"

At that I would have given anything to smash her head between two bricks, and everything in me at least wanted to tell her so in no uncertain terms. But she held all the high cards, and there was no point fighting with her. "I can't eat, strapped down like this," I said quietly. "I thought maybe —"

"That's your problem!" And she was gone. I knew then beyond a doubt, that the food being just out of reach was no accident. Someone else picked up the untouched tray later, but I didn't bother to comment.

It was no use yelling, I discovered later that night, and twice again the diarrhea caught up with me. By morning, I was not only filthy, but my buttocks and legs were burning with irritation. In addition I'd been stabbed with severe pains — the usual withdrawal pangs — all night long.

The next morning there were some new faces in the nursing crew, and after they'd cleaned me up — complaining bitterly the whole time — I got a piece of dry toast and a cup of cold coffee, with one hand freed enough to use it, and with a pillow to help prop me up on the flat bed surface.

Shortly afterward, I was unstrapped by a male attendant, given a pair of gray pajamas and a sorry-looking robe, and taken to another room, where I joined seven or eight other guys — all about as rough-looking as I must have been. The room was about twelve feet square, with benches along each wall. It was obvious we were locked in when attendants weren't there with us.

I didn't feel like talking to anyone, but I listened, and I soon figured out the others were there for various reasons — accidents while under the influence of drugs or alcohol . . . mental problems such as I'd experienced . . . even a sex offender who seemed to enjoy talking about his exploits. It was, all in all, a pitiful group.

After half-an-hour or so, several attendants came, and we were yelled at pretty good, as though we were criminals. I wondered again why I'd ever volunteered to come here. The life I'd been living was wretched enough, to be sure, but it didn't hold a candle to this!

"All right, you guys, come on!" The gruff voice brought back my Army days. "Move it!"

We were marched to another building where we were put into another room, doors secured again, and a long wait began until we were called out individually for X-rays, blood and urine tests, and other routines. Toward noon we were taken back to our cells, but this time, although I was locked in, I wasn't strapped to that disgraceful excuse for a bed. I was free to bash my head against the walls of the padded cell, and that was exactly what I felt like doing. I began to make plans for escape.

But things weren't quite so bad after I'd eaten my lunch — the first decent food I'd had in days. And that afternoon, I was transferred to an open ward — still under strict supervision and control, but nothing like the jailhouse misery of solitary confinement, even though there were barred windows all around us. So I put aside, for the moment, my plans to slip away. I couldn't forget that I'd come here of my own free will, seeking help. If help was forthcoming, I'd stick it out.

On the following day, Jeanie and a friend came to visit me, and we had a half-hour chat. I felt worse than ever after they'd gone, for I could sense their pity, and I didn't exactly enjoy a conversation based on commiseration. I was glad when Jeanie said they'd be going to San Diego when they left, and didn't know when they'd return. It was bad enough having to feel sorry for myself; it was worse having someone else feel sorry for me, even though I'd sought that kind of attention much of my life.

Several days later when I was beginning to get over the horrendous withdrawal symptoms I was abruptly called to a doctor's office. I was told I was to be discharged because there was nothing further they could do for me. Since they hadn't done anything for me in the first place, that didn't make much sense, but I wasn't about to question it. I wanted out more than they wanted me in, that was for sure. And because I'd always run away when things were bad, that's what I did now. Within an hour after I left the Los Angeles County Hospital, I was on the road, thumbing it to Seattle again.

Once there I realized how useless it would be to check in with my mom and stepfather. I'd just get thrown out again, as I'd been before, so why bother?

I was feeling mighty low, wandering along the street in the drizzling rain, wishing there was some way out of my misery-filled existence. Then I saw a familiar sign: two words that were among the few I'd been able to read all my life, even before I started in school. It was on a big building, and knowing this was an organization that had, indeed, helped many a down-and-outer, I decided to check in at the Alcoholics Anonymous' meeting. It couldn't hurt; maybe it would help.

They were having a dance upstairs, so I dragged myself up there, walked inside, and sat down at a table. Everyone seemed to be having a fine time, so I gave it a try, and asked one of the ladies to dance with me. But it wasn't any fun. The drugs I'd started taking again had lost their edge, and I was in almost constant pain. So I sat down again after one dance.

Tormented, twisted, I felt like my entire body was a dungeon, and somewhere inside, I was locked in and trying to get out. I couldn't sit still, so I got up and headed toward the bathroom, and once there I found a high open window on the left, and from deep within me, I heard a voice.

"Now's a good time!" it said. "There's no one around, and you can jump out that window!"

So I climbed up on the toilet, and got into the window, which was probably three feet high and about two feet wide. It was like crawling through a porthole on a ship. I looked down, and it was a long ways, probably three stories, to the sidewalk.

"This is a good time to do it!" the voice urged me on. "It's late — there's nobody around!" The voice didn't say it, but I knew I'd be leaving a sordid world filled with fear, loneliness, depression, self-pity . . . the addict's world. I didn't hesitate. I edged myself out of the window and was just ready to tip over into the void beneath when someone grabbed my legs from behind.

"No!" I screamed. "Let me go!"

I squirmed and fought in anger, but I was caught in a vise-like grip. Try as I would — and I really wanted to die, so I tried with all my strength — I couldn't break that man's hold on me. He, too, was yelling, and yanking back on me at the same time. The noise brought others on the run, and their combined weight finally loosened my grip on the windowsill and we all tumbled to the floor, where the others held me fast.

"Get the police!" someone ordered, and until they came, I was held tight. First came the rescue squad, then the regular patrolmen. The familiar click of metal on my wrists told me I was on a one-way trip to another of those joyful places I'd learned to abhor — a jail cell.

But I was wrong. With the handcuffs still on, the cops led me down a long hallway at the Seattle State Hospital, first to the reception desk, and then to the emergency ward. And there, they stuck me in a small, sparsely furnished room, took off the cuffs, and locked me in. Before long, a doctor came in, looked at some papers in his hand, and then sat down on one of the two wooden chairs in the room.

He didn't waste any words. "Why did you want to kill yourself, Gary?" He was just matter-of-fact about it, like he'd asked me why I liked to eat ice cream cones.

I didn't know what to say. I didn't care if I said anything at all. I felt like my mind had deserted me, like I just couldn't face any responsibilities any longer — even the responsibilities of eating and sleeping or scoring on the drug scene to feed my habit.

"I wanted to die!" I said. "If I get out of this hospital, I'm going to kill myself!"

He smiled a sad smile and shook his head. "Then we'll just have to put you away for a while, Gary, until you snap out of it," he said. And then, expressing a hope I couldn't share, "Maybe we can convince you life really is worth living."

He left, only to return a few minutes later with some attendants who took me up to the third floor and locked me in another padded cell. I could almost have closed my eyes and I'd have been right back in Los Angeles, except here they didn't bother to strap me down. There was the same hard bed, the same wadding-lined walls, the same feeling of helplessness I'd run away from only a few days before. And they were going to convince me life was worth living.

As it always was, the first night was nothing short of hell itself. The super-pain of withdrawal frayed my nerves raw, and I would gladly have killed myself there in that cell if I could have found a way. But there was nothing to do except sweat it out.

The next day, there was medication, more questions and notes taken on my case. But they left me in the cubicle — alone, friendless, made to feel I wasn't worthy of associating with anyone else, sane or otherwise.

Three days later, they put me in a ward with others, but that didn't help my outlook much, except show me I wasn't the only one with a problem. One guy in the ward decided shortly after I was assigned there that I had a telegraph office in my bed, and he wanted me to telegraph his mother a message. I tried to ignore him, but he began getting angry.

"Look, man, if you don't send my mom a telegram, I'll wreck your whole place, and you won't send anything. I'll —"

"Okay, I'll send it!" I agreed. "What do you want to say?"

And while he mumbled a lot of unintelligible garbage, I sat there and pretended I was tapping a telegraph key to send the message to his mother. Then, just to keep him off my back, I made him be quiet while I picked up a return wire from her.

"She says, 'Hang in there,' " I told him. "She says, 'Do what the doctors tell you, and everything's going to be cool.' " I stopped to think a minute. He was clinging to every word, a smile on his lips. "She says, 'Everyone here at home is fine, and we all send our love.' "

He came and put his arms around me, and there were tears in his eyes. "Gee, thanks, buddy!" he choked. "That's the best news I've had in a month!"

Somewhere, deep down, I had a good feeling. I'd managed to help someone, even if it did involve playing a couple of tricks with the truth. It was a feeling of gratification I could never remember running up against before, and I liked it. Maybe that doctor had been right; maybe life *was* worth living.

* * * *

But when they let me out onto the streets again a few days later, there was only one thing on my mind. I wasn't in pain any more, but my entire body cried out for more drugs. I could taste them in my mouth. The eternal craving was there; I could not shake it, even if I'd wanted to. So I went and bought my cough medicine — terpin hydrate with codeine. And when I'd gotten loaded, I wandered around until I found an old friend, Bill, who was always willing to share his shelter with me. It seemed I resembled Bill's younger brother, who'd died of pneumonia, and Bill had taken a special liking to me. So, I stayed loaded and lonely at his place for a couple of days.

As I'd done many times before, I hitchhiked to a suburb of Seattle, White Center, but we always called it Rat City. It was a place I knew well, for I'd been in and out of every bar and drugstore there countless times. This time, I found a bar and started drinking beer, still feeling sorry for myself, wondering how I could find a quick way of killing myself. It didn't take long. There was one swift scheme; I'd go out in the street and jump in front of a car.

So I walked out of the bar and crossed the boulevard to a side street, where I knew a lot of cars drag-raced. I walked far enough down to make sure they'd have plenty of speed, then I hid behind a telephone pole, waiting for the fastest car to come smoking by. It was easy to hide. At one hundred and thirty-five pounds and five feet, eleven and a half inches, I was so skinny no one could see me behind that pole.

Then I saw it — a red car, roaring down the street. "This is the one!" I told myself, poising to leap.

Now! I thought I'd timed it perfectly. The piercing scream of tires on pavement filled my ears. The red monster swerved just in time. He'd missed me. There I was, sprawled on the roadway, egg on my face again . . . another Gary Fisher failure.

The driver was out of his car by now and bending over me. "Man, what are you trying to do — kill yourself?"

"Yes," I mumbled. "I want to die! I'm a drug addict — there's no use going on!"

"Well, hell!" he said. "Why'd you pick me? I got enough problems of my own. I got a family to take care of." He glared at me for a moment. "You want to kill yourself, go do it in front of somebody else's car. Don't pick on me!"

Slowly I got up and brushed myself off, and as if I had something contagious, the driver turned and jumped into his red car, laying rubber all the way down the street. It dawned on me he'd probably call the cops, so I took off running. I couldn't stand the thought of another padded or barred cell. No way!

Whenever I was totally confused, like then, I thought of my mother, who'd always done her best to help. So I headed for her house. Empty. Maybe she was at my uncle's, nearby. I was right. My reception there was cordial but strained. After we'd passed the time of day a while, and they asked me how I was, I went upstairs to the bathroom, and without really looking for it, found a half-full bottle of whiskey in the medicine cabinet. Minutes later, the bottle was empty.

When you mix a combination like codeine (in the terpin

hydrate I used), beer, and then whiskey, it adds up to one thing: dynamite. I went back down stairs in a rage, headed for the kitchen, and found a butcher knife. I was going to stab myself — the mixture I'd downed brought me the courage. But then my uncle entered the kitchen.

"Hold it, Gary!" he warned. "Give me that knife!"

I didn't hesitate. I'd give it to him, all right — square in the stomach! I lunged at him, but I was drunk and he wasn't, and he got out of the way, dodging out of the house with me shouting at his heels.

Then I turned back in. I'd take on my stepfather next; there were still some scores I hadn't settled with him. But when I got back in, brandishing the knife, my aunt — whom I had always loved a lot because she'd been good to me — met me.

"Give me the knife, Gary," she said quietly. "It's mine, you know." And she held out her hand.

"No!" I said. "I got to use it first!"

"I don't want you using my knife," my aunt stated in a calm voice. "I need my knife, Gary. Give it to me."

Her words confused me. Maybe it was her knife. Let's see — I'd gotten it from her kitchen. Yes, it was her knife. I'd have to give it back to her. So I did.

"Thank you, Gary." She patted my arm. "I'll just put it away." And she moved toward the kitchen.

I sat down, holding my head in my hands. I was muddled; I was embarrassed; I was shattered. Everything I did or tried to do went haywire.

"Come on, Gary," my mother said then. "We'll take you downtown."

Grateful for any positive action, I nodded. "Sure," I said. "Thanks."

We left worried looks behind us as we went out the door, and a half-hour later, I was back on the streets, clutching the ten-dollar-bill my mother had slipped me, and wondering where I could con another bottle of cough medicine from an unsuspecting pharmacist.

The loathsome memory of what I'd done at my aunt and uncle's house dogged my footsteps, so there was only one thing to do — put as many miles as I could between me and their house. I headed for Los Angeles a couple of hours after my folks let me off in downtown Seattle.

When I got to Hollywood, I got drunk, but the cops decided there was a better place for me — the Lincoln Heights Jail, known on the streets as the "Glass House for Drunks." It was quite a place — old, impossible to maintain properly, always filled with the dregs of society. And that wasn't all. It was filled with cockroaches, too — big ones, the size of your thumb, crawling all over everything. The best thing you could say about it was it was a roof over your head.

After a three or four-day stay in there I decided my welcome back to Los Angeles wasn't really all I'd hoped for, so when they let me out, Seattle seemed once again like a faraway land of plenty where I could get myself straightened out. I would hit the road again; they could keep their old Los Angeles jail.

I had a stop to make first, of course — a little liquor store where I bought a fifth of wine. I drank it all. It would make the trip more bearable.

But when I got to Figueroa Street, a main thoroughfare I expected to lead me away from the city, it started raining. It wasn't just a drizzle; it was some kind of deluge, and I walked along Figueroa getting wetter by the minute. No one would stop to pick me up, probably because they thought I was nothing but a bum. I probably did look pretty bad — three or four days of beard, ragged, dirty, wearing an old beat-up Army surplus overcoat that almost dragged the ground. So I just kept on walking, holding out my thumb in a futile hope that someone would take pity on me.

Between Riverside Drive and San Fernando Road, there's a bridge across the Los Angeles River on Figueroa Street, and by the time I got to the center of that bridge, I'd had it. No one was going to give me a ride anyway, and there was a five hundred foot drop to the concrete bed of the river and with only eight inches or so of water down there, I'd splatter all over the place. I might as well jump.

I stood there on the top rail of that bridge looking down, and my whole mixed-up life flooded into my mind. What was I living for? Nothing! What was I now? A junkie, a drunk. Was I worth anything to anybody? Not so you could notice it. Did I have anything to look forward to? Not that I could think of . . . even another blast of drugs didn't exactly appeal to me at that point. I'd make the leap, and that would be that. I started crying softly to myself, because there was no one else to cry for me.

Then I heard the squeal of tires, a sound burned into my brain from two previous occasions when I'd tried to do myself in.

"Hey, man — hold it!" The voice was friendly, like maybe he really wanted to help. "Hang on a minute! You don't want to do that!"

I turned to see a young man of perhaps my own age, climbing up the bridge railing to where I was. He'd gotten out of a red car and I wondered why red cars kept popping up in my life. My friend stopped, halfway up.

"Man, you don't want to jump off of here," he told me. "We got a swinging party up the road a piece, up in the canyon. Come on down, and we'll go up there. Get you a real fine chick! How about it?"

It sounded good, but I didn't move. How did I know he was telling it to me straight?

"Hey, man, you can't give up now," he went on. "You're just getting a good start. Come on down — come on with us!"

I finally found my tongue. "No use going on," I explained. "Life's just not worth it anymore."

"Oh, man, you got it all wrong!" he said. "You just got off on the wrong foot! Come on down, and we'll make the party and I'll show you what I mean. It's a groove!"

By this time I could see cars lined up for a mile down the road, honking because my friend had stopped in the middle of the bridge. There were two other guys, I could see, waiting at the car, watching the two of us. And behind them, others had gotten out of their cars and were looking at me. I hadn't counted on all this audience, and it bothered me. If I was going to do it, I wanted to do it by myself, not in front of half of Los Angeles.

So I climbed down. Besides, going to a party sounded good. I could use a new groove. But the minute we reached the pavement, a swarm of black-and-whites came roaring in from every direction. Someone had squealed, and here I was, busted again. I had my hands in place for the cuffs even before the officer had them out of their leather case.

My benefactor friend did his best. "He's okay, now," he pleaded with the cops. "He'll be all right. We'll take care of him."

The cop snickered. "Oh, sure," he said. "He'll be all right, but he's our problem now — not yours. Thanks just the same."

"Hey, we'll follow you," my new-found friend said. "Like — maybe we can bail him out."

With a shrug, the policeman snapped on the cuffs. "Up to you," he said.

They pushed me into the back seat of the police car, and back we went to where I'd started — the Lincoln Heights jail. The guy who'd talked me down off the bridge and his two buddies stood by while they booked me, but the authorities wouldn't let me go, and my new friends went away empty-handed. As for me, I went through the booking process, was given a stale bologna sandwich, rolled up the worn-out mattress on my back again, and went up into the drunk tank. There were thirty-two bunks, and at least twice that many guys in the tank — sprawled all over the floor. I could hardly find a space to put my mattress on.

Next morning, they led me before a lady judge, the only time I'd ever faced a female in court. It wasn't really that much different at the start, because a familiar question was the first thing that came up.

"Why do you want to kill yourself, Gary Fisher?"

I was afraid to tell her I was using drugs, for fear I might get an endless siege in the clink, or possibly even worse, a long term in a mental ward somewhere. So I took the easy way out.

"I'm an alcoholic," I said. "I just got out of the service a little while back, and I was on the way home to see my mother, and —" I gave her my best head-hanging act. "Well, I just slipped and got drunk and — I couldn't face life any longer."

"Well, Gary," she said earnestly, "I'm going to sentence you to seven days in jail, to give you a chance to dry out. Now — when you are out, I want you to go home to your mother, get yourself on the right road, and see if you can't straighten out your life. Have you heard of an organization called Alcoholics Anonymous?''

Heard of it? I was practically a charter member since I was three years old! But I didn't tell her that.

"Yes, ma'am," I said. "I've heard of them."

"Give them a chance to help you," the lady judge advised. And then, as though she'd spent too much time on my case already, "Good luck!"

I went back to Lincoln Heights for the seven days along with the cockroaches and the lushes. We could get all the doughnuts and candy we wanted, but there were never enough cigarettes, so I'd trade doughnuts and candy for smokes, and I got along pretty good, after the usual pains of withdrawal the first few days.

While I was there, one of the guys told me he was going to head for eastern Washington to pick fruit when he got out in a couple of weeks, so I figured that sounded like a good way for me to go, too. There had been nothing for me in the Los Angeles area, and even less in Seattle. Maybe what I needed was a whole new scene — outdoor work, fresh fruit to eat instead of pills. It might be worth a try.

I had time to think, for seven days. What a long ways down I'd come! All those attempts to kill myself, and I hadn't been able to get the job done. This last try was even splashed on the pages of the Los Angeles *Herald-Examiner* — one of my jailmates saw the article and showed it to me. For the first time, I faced an inescapable conclusion: Something was stopping me from doing away with myself. I'd had several very close calls, but they'd been just that. Close. Was there really a God up there somewhere, maybe with His hand on me? Was my old grandmother right? She'd used to tell my mother many years before that I would one day be used of God, if only I would let the Lord fill my emptiness. But of course I'd never listened to her.

Chapter Eight

By the time I got to eastern Washington, the 1963 fruit picking season was just about over, although I did find a few days' work along the Snake River, not far from where it empties into the Columbia. I was able to work enough to satisfy my needs, which mainly consisted of a four-ounce bottle of terpin hydrate every other day. I didn't care very much what happened the rest of the time; if I found enough to eat, well and good. If I didn't, it didn't matter, for I was loaded on the codeine in the cough medicine on a continuous basis.

For the next several months I just wandered from place to place in the northwest. It was new territory for me, and I could get all the terpin hydrate I needed, because no one knew me. I could claim I needed it for my cough which, I would warn dubious druggists, would turn into an asthma attack if I let it go too long.

How, or exactly when, I wound up in Caribou Creek, Idaho, a little town of about 3,000 in the southeast corner of the state, I am uncertain. But once there, I met a girl who was friendly and seemed interested in helping me. That, of course, was all I needed — I'd been searching all my life for someone to love me, and while her friendship was not by any means the deep love I longed for, the mere fact she seemed concerned for my well-being made me reach out to receive whatever assistance she could offer.

Perhaps Betty was unusually sympathetic because she herself needed someone else's consideration. She was the mother of a three-month-old baby boy, whose father had disappeared. And in a small town like that, an unattached mother is not entirely welcome in the finer circles of society. So it was perhaps natural she'd want to help someone else who didn't quite fit in.

Anyway, Betty welcomed me to her parents' home, and they, too, seemed eager to help a poor drifter who was down on his luck, and into the drug scene as well. I didn't pull any punches with them. I told them I was hooked on codeine and the only way I could keep going was to take terpin hydrate. And for once, instead of rejection, I received a generously warm welcome.

"Gary, we'll do what we can to help you," Betty's father told me.

"Let me get you something to eat," her mother added. "You look starved."

I probably did look pretty bad, and I was content to accept whatever these kindly people were willing to provide. For a time, I simply enjoyed their hospitality, picking up my terpin hydrate when I needed it, and staying loaded day after day. To my surprise, they didn't interfere. They wouldn't go so far as to get the stuff for me, but they didn't object to my taking it.

My routine was to sleep till about noon in the small room they gave me, then get up, eat something, and wander around town in the late afternoon to see if there was any work I could do. But a small town like Caribou Creek didn't have much to offer in the way of work for an unskilled person whose habits, even to the naive, appeared questionable.

So I'd go back to the Hastings family in total disillusionment, which meant I'd need another bottle of terpin hydrate. One Sunday the family went to church and, perhaps thinking they were doing the right thing, locked me in my little bedroom. They probably felt I wouldn't wake up until they'd returned, anyway.

But toward noon, I did awaken and tried to open the bedroom door, only to find it fastened tight. I went into a rage — who the hell did they think they were? — and smashed a hole in the door with my fist. Then, because I still couldn't open it I finally broke it open by slamming my shoulder against it. The door was pretty well splintered before I was through.

When the family finally came home I was in the kitchen

frying myself some eggs. Betty's father saw the broken door almost immediately. "Hey — what happened?"

I shrugged. "Crazy door got locked some way," I explained. "I had to get out, so I — got out." I didn't feel any need to provide additional details.

Turning to his wife, Mr. Hastings said, "This young man's got to have help. See if you can get hold of Doctor Robertson."

Betty's mother telephoned, and the next thing I knew, the whole family was taking me to the doctor's office. It was only a short trip, but it seemed like forever, because no one said anything.

When we got to the doctor's office, Mr. and Mrs. Hastings had a private consultation with him before he talked to me. When they were through, he didn't waste much time on me. "Take one of these Mr. Fisher, when you get home, one after each meal, and one at bedtime," he told me, holding out an envelope with some pills in it. "I've given the Hastings a prescription for refills, if you need it." Then, with sort of an embarrassed smile, "And no more terpin hydrate — it's not really good for you."

He might as well have told a catfish no more swimming in muddy water. I took the envelope of pills, and when we got to the Hastings house, I did my duty and took one. I knew it was some kind of tranquilizer, and I was willing enough to take it, hoping it might indeed calm me down inside. But the pill was just like the doctor's parting advice, it had no effect.

I hitchhiked the thirty miles to Montpelier that afternoon and picked up a couple of bottles of terpin hydrate from a pharmacist who hadn't seen me before. I was back at the Hastings place in Caribou Creek before nine that night, and if they suspected where I'd gone and what I'd gone for, they said nothing.

A few days later, I awoke at mid-morning to find both my arms tied securely to the iron bedstead with strips of denim cloth. Furious, I started hollering, and then I recalled I'd told Betty the night before to tie me down if they were going to be gone from the house, because I was out of tranquilizers and my regular drugs, and I didn't want to go out and get into more trouble. She'd agreed, telling me at the same time they would be gone until about noon the next day. So here I was, on a leash, like a mad dog, waiting for them to bring me a refill on my prescription.

At first, I was determined to break loose, but thinking about it, I realized I'd asked for this kind of treatment. They'd be back before too long, I told myself, and until then, I'd relax, so I lay back on the bed. But I couldn't go to sleep, and for several hours, I let my mind wander back over the weeks and the months and the years that had brought me there.

Shortly the ramblings in my mind began to be replaced by physical pain — I could nearly always count on a migraine headache as the first sign that I was heading into withdrawal and needed another blast of terpin hydrate. For a while, I managed to push the pain aside, but with the passing of time this became impossible. *I had to get some terpin hydrate.*

I couldn't extricate myself from the bonds, so there was just one thing to do — my feet were free and I dragged the bed with me as far as the doorway. Once there, in the frenzy that only a junkie desperate for a fix knows, I managed to knock the bed apart and drag the bedpost with me into the other rooms, leaving a mangled clutter behind. I knew I couldn't very well drag the bed-frame down the street, so I sat in the living room and waited. ". . . . back around noon," Betty had said. At four o'clock, she and her mother and the baby returned. Her dad arrived soon after.

They all blew their stacks, and I blew mine right back, telling them what I thought for keeping me tied up like some kind of animal, even if I had asked them to. A lot of bitter things were said, and finally they cut away the denim strips, leaving me free to head for the drugstore and some terpin hydrate. It was late January and there was snow in the air, but I didn't notice; I was still burning inside from some of the things that had been said.

Nor had I cooled down any when I returned later that night, one bottle of terpin hydrate in my gut and another in my pocket. Little was said when I came in and I headed for my bedroom, only to find the springs and mattress on the floor because I'd ruined the bedstead. Instead of exploding, I laid down on the mattress and began to take a fresh look at the Hastings.

These people, I felt, were not capable of love; that was obvious from the way they had treated me. What a tragedy that Betty's small baby boy — three months old — had to grow up in an atmosphere like that. Certainly, the baby could never have a decent life with that sort of family environment.

I'd leaned on this family because they seemed to want to help, but after today's treatment, it was obvious there was no love for me in their hearts. And that poor baby . . . he, too, needed love which they simply weren't capable of providing him. It occurred to me then how much the baby and I had in common. We were outcasts, unwanted, and unloved.

But there *was* someone who could give the baby the love he needed and wasn't getting, someone who had never gotten the love he should have had, either. Maybe I couldn't receive love from others, but at least I could give it.

It was easy to slip quietly into Betty's room later on that night and bundle up the baby. I figured it would probably be down to at least ten above zero outside, so I was careful to wrap the baby in several blankets. And I took a heavy coat from Mr. Hastings' closet to shield myself against the frigid Idaho air. I didn't know exactly what I was going to do. All I knew was the baby and I could exchange our love — a far better situation then existed for either of us now.

It was only a short distance to the highway, but even those few blocks made me realize how cold it was. I was glad I'd bundled the baby up and he seemed to be sleeping through it all. On the highway leading to Pocatello we didn't have to wait long until a guy rolled to a stop and invited us in. He didn't seem to wonder about my being out in the night with a baby; he took us to the first town, Bancroft, and dropped us off there. I had no trouble finding a bar, so I walked in, sat down on one of the stools, laid the baby on the bar, and ordered a beer.

I was pleased when a couple came over from their table and seemed interested in the bundle on the bar. Someone was paying attention to us.

"That baby is certainly tiny," the lady said after taking a peek inside the blankets. "Is there anything we can do to help?"

"Well," I said, "I don't know." I wasn't sure what she had

on her mind — help or trouble!

Then the man spoke. "Do you and the baby have a place to stay tonight?"

I saw no reason to lie. "No."

"Tell you what," the lady said. "You can come and stay in our trailer — it's parked behind our house. We keep the heater on anyway, to keep it from freezing up, and you'll be warm and snug there."

"Fine!" I said. Already things were turning out just great for the baby and me. We'd only been gone an hour or so, and we had a good place to spend the night.

We drove a couple of blocks to their little home, and sure enough, there was a small house trailer in back of it. There was a nice bed in one end of the trailer, and I kept the baby on it with me. He'd know it was going to be just us two from then on — each one to love the other. Everything was going to be fine.

The next morning, quite early, there was a loud knock on the trailer door. I got up and opened it, and there stood a big man with a cowboy hat on, holding a shotgun in one hand and some chains in the other.

"Are you Gary Fisher?" he asked.

"Yes, I am."

"I have a warrant for your arrest, for kidnapping. Step out of the trailer, sir."

I couldn't remember anyone ever calling me "Sir" before, but it didn't matter. Apparently something had gone wrong with my efforts to bring a new life to the baby and me.

"Turn around, please." The sheriff had a voice to match his size. I did as I was told, automatically putting my hands behind my back. I'd been busted so many times it was almost instinct.

When the handcuffs attached to the sheriff's chains were snapped on, I could hear the baby begin crying from inside the trailer. All my hopes and dreams were shattered again. The shackles went on my legs next with a chain going from them to the cuffs. I could only move my feet a few inches at a time. The sheriff put me in the patrol car. He returned to the trailer, got the baby, and handed him to a lady I'd never seen before. She'd come out of the house while I was being taken to the car.

The sheriff didn't waste any time traveling the sixteen miles back to Caribou Creek, and once there, he loosened the shackles on my legs, letting them dangle while I walked up the stairs to the tiny jail cell. The only person I saw the next two days was the lady — probably the sheriff's wife — who brought me a simple meal three times a day. And as usual, I didn't care whether I ate or not, because the pains of withdrawal had taken over by mid-day and I was in abject misery from then on.

On the third day, about nine-thirty in the morning, a deputy sheriff led me to a downstairs room in the same building for my court hearing. I couldn't have cared less what happened at that point. I was practically wild with distress from drug withdrawal; what was left of my mind was fogged with torment.

The deputy opened the door and when I walked through it I saw a large oval table with a judge sitting at one end, and beside him was a man I recognized as the doctor I'd been taken to see a few days earlier. On the other side sat Mrs. Hastings and Betty. I was given a place at the opposite end.

"This is an official hearing into the case of Gary Fisher, charged with kidnap of a three-month-old child," the judge pronounced slowly. Then, addressing me directly, "Gary Fisher, you may speak up for yourself and tell me exactly how you feel about your situation. I'd like to hear from you now."

I tried to get my mind in order so I could defend myself, but it wasn't easy. Finally, I was able to squeeze out a few words. "I don't feel I did anything wrong," I told the judge. "I wasn't trying to hurt the baby — I just wanted to give the child the love I think he should have. I — felt I could give him that love."

"You felt the baby wasn't loved by the Hastings family?"

"That's right, your honor," I said. "I wanted to give it the love it wasn't getting."

The judge nodded. "All right," he said. "Doctor Robertson?"

"Yes," the doctor nodded his head. "I saw Mr. Fisher in my office at the request of the Hastings family some time ago. I feel this is a case where drug addiction leaves no choice other than special treatment."

He paused, looking first at me, then the Hastings pair, and

the judge. "His mind is completely gone," he said. "I believe he should be committed until he has been wholly cured."

The judge nodded, and my mind cleared enough to wonder: *How long is that? And where will they put me?*

Then the judge turned to Betty. "May we have your opinion, please?"

Betty didn't look at me when she spoke. She just hung her head and talked so softly it was hard to make out the words. "We wanted to help him," she began, "but he turned out to be really mean. He — knocked a door down once — like an animal. Then he —" she paused and almost broke into tears. "He — stole my baby!"

"All right," the judge said quietly. "Mrs. Hastings?"

"He's crazy!" she burst out. "He's hooked on all kinds of drugs. He needs to be put away!"

The judge nodded, but Mrs. Hastings wasn't through. "If he's turned loose now, I just don't know what would happen. He might even kill someone," she added.

Again the judge nodded, then he looked over the notes he'd made on a pad of paper and turned to me.

"Gary Fisher, will you please rise."

I stood up.

"Gary Fisher — I sentence you to the State Hospital South, a mental institution for the criminally insane, for whatever period of time it takes you to get well."

I could only stand there and stare at him. This was no voluntary situation like I'd experienced in Los Angeles, no spur-of-the-moment deal like I'd gone through in Seattle. This was commitment to a mental institution. For how long? Maybe months . . . maybe years. I stood and stared at the judge, my mouth hanging open in sheer dread of what I had to face.

But his Honor wasn't through. "If it takes a year, that's how long you'll be there," the judge said. "If it takes twenty years, that's how long you'll be there." He sighed, shaking his head. "If it takes the rest of your life, that's how long — you'll be there." I could barely hear his last three words.

Chapter Nine

The uncertainty of the next twenty-four hours was a new realm of Hell. Not knowing what a real mental hospital would be like — I'd been only in mental wards of general hospitals before that — and fearing the worst, I could only lie on the pallet in the jail cell and worry about what was to come. My mind echoed with the judge's pronouncement . . . "for whatever period of time it takes you to get well." As excruciating as the physical pain of drug withdrawal was, at least I'd been that route before, and I knew it would end, but the prospect of facing the unknown in an insane asylum possibly forever was more than I could bear. By the time the sheriff drove me, chained from head to toe, the next morning to the state hospital, I was half-mad from fear.

Although I'd never actually seen places like San Quentin or Folsom Prison, except in movies, State Hospital South at Blackfoot, Idaho, looked exactly as I'd have imagined them to look. Its ominous gray walls loomed eighteen to twenty feet high; and there was a watch tower in the middle, silhouetted against the darkening sky. When I heard that first door shut behind me, I felt like I was giving up life itself. I was sure there would be no way out of that place for me.

There were several more locked doors to go through, then a padded cell, not unlike those I'd been in before. But at least I wasn't strapped down. I could move around within the cell, and even though I knew my chances of becoming a free man again were dim, I sat down to think about what I could do to get away from this place. If there was a way, I'd find it!

I have no idea how long I was confined in the cell. But somewhere along the way — a day, maybe several days later — I was moved to an open ward. It was a good thing I'd been exposed to erratic behavior the years before; I could recognize almost immediately what the pattern was here. Homosexuality was obviously the key social situation. The first night, there was a little party in the ward — everyone had saved up all the shaving lotion they could get their hands on and dumped it together to make a potent punch that could knock anyone into oblivion.

I didn't sleep at all that first night; I was too scared. The minute the lights were turned out, there was a shifting from one bed to another, like musical chairs, except there were two men to a bed now. I pushed my bed up against the wall and lay with my back against it so I could fend off anyone trying to molest me.

Next day, I asked one young man who seemed to be a little more sensible than some of the others if there was any hope of getting out of this place.

"Easy," he grinned. "All you got to do is get into the program. That's all it takes."

"Okay," I said. "What's the program? What do I do?"

"Talk to the psychiatrist," he explained. "Play along with them. Take the pills," he looked around and lowered his voice, "and take the treatment."

"The treatment?" I asked. "What's that?"

He held out his hands in front of him, formed them into fists close together, and then split them quickly apart. "Shock!" he said simply. "You got to go for electric shock!"

Later that day, I was called out of the ward and led to a big room where there was only a desk with a couple of chairs. A doctor wearing a white smock and carrying a clipboard with a lot of papers came in then and started asking me questions. I didn't realize at first that he was probably a psychiatrist, but as the questions progressed, I finally got the picture.

"Do you love your mother, Gary?"

"I guess so," I replied. "If you can love an alcoholic."

His eyebrows raised. "I see," he said. "Did she neglect you because of her — alcoholic trouble?"

"You better believe it!" I said.

He made some notes on his pad. "Do you feel you're ugly, Gary?"

I thought a minute. "Yeah, I suppose so," I said, not knowing what answer might convince him I'd been sent to the wrong place. "I never have been much on looks."

More notes on his paper. "Gary, do you feel you're not as good as other people?" Again I gave it some thought.

"I've had some problems," I admitted. "There are times. . ." I didn't know just what more I should add.

"How about hobbies?" he asked me then. "Why don't you get a hobby? Keep your mind occupied. How'd you like to build model airplanes?"

That did it; the answer just popped out: "I'd probably get loaded on the glue!"

Another eyebrow twitch from the man in the white coat. "Why do you take drugs, Gary?"

There wasn't any point in kidding around. "To get loaded," I replied. "What else?"

"Loaded — you like being loaded?"

"Not especially. I just — can't help it. It's a — a —"

"Compulsion?"

"Yeah, I guess you'd call it that. I get this craving, and I can't stay away from —"

"Gary, we'd like to give you some special treatments here at the hospital," the doctor interrupted. "You're not required to take them, of course, but we believe from experience they'll do you some good."

I nodded, waiting.

"With your permission, we'll schedule your first treatment for tomorrow morning. All right?"

I figured I knew what he was talking about, and I figured it might as well be out in the open. "You mean electric shock treatments?"

Eyebrows up again. "The word gets around fast, doesn't it?" he said. Then, "Yes, we think shock treatments can help in cases like yours."

I had no idea, of course, what shock treatments involved. But

I wanted to get out of this place, and I had to "get into the program." Not only that, I really did want help; if this doctor believed shock treatments would help me, then that was for me.

"Fine," I said. "Let's have at it!"

Had I but known. . . Perhaps the fright of facing the treatment was worst. The next morning, I lined up with a bunch of others, to wait for my treatment, and I began to wonder what I'd let myself in for. When others would be wheeled out on their stretchers, they looked like they'd been blown clear out of existence — tongues hanging out, obviously unconscious, but with their eyeballs wide open . . . they were frightening!

Waiting in line was like waiting to go to the electric chair. And finally, it was my turn. I walked on jittery legs to the special table waiting for me. They laid me out on it, strapping my arms down to the sides. Then a strap across my chest, one over my legs and then they drew a sheet over me. I was reminded of how they pull a sheet up over the head of a person who has died. Was this to be my fate? Had it all come down to this? I lay there shaking with fear, recoiling at the slight but unmistakable odor of burning flesh.

Next came a wide rubber band around my head, with flat metal staves in it fitting against my temples, and some sort of jelly-like ointment smeared on them. Then they had me open my mouth and inserted a rubber piece like a boxer uses, to keep me from biting my tongue. A hypodermic went into my arm, and the preliminary routine was through. By now, I was numb with fear, especially seeing half-a-dozen attendants standing by; I could only guess they were there to hold me down.

The practice, as I was given to understand it, was to shoot about 120 volts of electric current for about three-tenths of a second. That didn't sound so bad, but when they turned the juice on, it felt like an iron ball had exploded in my head! I could feel the impact for a split instant, and I could feel my body arch with the force of the shock. Then, blackout.

The next thing I knew, I was sitting in front of a table beside two little old ladies, with a cup of coffee and a doughnut in front of me. I vaguely recalled that I'd seen one of those ladies being wheeled out of the room — her tongue hanging loose, her eyes bulging, her body stiff — just before I'd gone in. She looked okay, now, and she smiled at me.

"Have some coffee," she urged. "It tastes pretty good, after — the hellfire."

Hellfire. That was a good word for it. I hadn't been sure I'd ever come out of that room alive. But I had, though I wasn't at all sure I ever wanted to go back. "You got to get into the program," I'd been told. I was into it all right, all the way. Maybe that *was* the only way to get out of this place, and if it was — well, I'd survived shock treatment number one; maybe I could stand number two. . .

In the days that followed, I got used to even that incredible routine. I came to know what to expect from the smelly, dirty, withdrawn patients around me. With some, the most they could accomplish was to sit and stare at the wall. Others appeared to be reasonably normal. It was an ordinary occurrence — in which I, too, joined — to tell the attendants and the doctors and anyone else in sight that "I'm okay — I shouldn't be in here!" They would all smile and agree and go on about their business.

There were more talks with the psychiatrist — the shrink, as everyone jokingly called him. Other pill-pushers got into the picture, too — sometimes with the same questions, sometimes different ones. There were a couple of attempts at hypnosis, but they didn't seem to get anywhere, so the doctors gave up on that. There were more shock treatments — every other day or so. And there were the sleepless nights of fear that I'd be attacked and subjected to the ravages of homosexual abuse, about which the attendants were apparently unable — or unwilling — to do anything.

There was little to do in the way of recreation. Some patients would sit for hours in front of the television set, and it was impossible to tell whether they were really aware of what was going on.

We were just a group of rumpled, useless, wrecked bodies. As for me, I was quite confused as to what it was all about for the first twenty-four hours or so after a shock treatment. After that, most of my time would be spent in anxious dread of the next shock session; I couldn't get my mind on much of anything else.

At times, I felt, as did most of the others, a total abandonment of hope . . . the best I could see ahead was the steady erosion of what was left of my humanity. Yet, at other times, I'd grit my teeth with determination to see this senseless existence through, so that somehow, I could get away from it.

There was a dance a week or so after my arrival, and not knowing any better, I decided to go. I went into this big room, and the door was locked behind me, so there was no way to leave till the dance was over. And what an affair that was!

From the time I got inside, I got plenty of exercise, for there were little old ladies coming up to me wanting to dance, and I wasn't quite ready to tackle that job. So I started running from corner to corner to get away, and I never did get a chance to dance with someone I'd picked out, because these old-timers kept on my trail. I learned later that the only people who went to the dances were the far-out mental cases; those with any sense left to them wisely stayed away.

Some of those dancing were simply standing and holding each other, without movement. Others were dancing by themselves — heads high in the air, lost in their own fuzzy world. And one poor soul was standing at the rear, as far as possible away from the moaning record player, automatically saluting the wall at two-minute intervals.

One woman dancing by herself suddenly stopped, and without warning, began stripping off her clothes and flinging them across the floor. She'd gotten everything off but her panties by the time two attendants quietly came up and bundled her into a robe, leading her away from the dance floor. And all the time, the twilight zone music filtered through the inhuman monotone that permeated the room.

I was glad I hadn't agreed to dance with any of the older women who'd chased me, when I saw one of them attempt to prompt a sex act with her partner right on the dance floor. She, too, was led away, and I couldn't help feeling sorry for these poor tortured souls. No matter how bad off I might be, I hadn't yet deteriorated to the extent that some of these had. As long as I could stand the shock treatments, I felt, maybe there was hope for my release.

I endured the mental and physical abuse of shock treatment — desirable and effective though it may be in treating mental illness, I can't describe it in any other terms — for what seemed to be a period of weeks, perhaps months. The pattern changed little: fear heaped on fear as I awaited my turn on the table . . . the involuntary shudder as the band went round my head and the restraining straps were buckled into place . . . the thunderbolt that wracked the body into a convulsive arch . . . the ebony void until at last my eyes would slowly flare open to rest on a long hall-like room with fifteen or twenty identical rolling beds, like slabs in a morgue. All strapped down, all covered with sheets, all lying there with tongues hanging out of deathpallored faces . . . zombies, one and all.

As we'd start to come out of the void, the men in white would unstrap us, and often two or three old ladies or men would walk around holding on to one another's hands like little children, before finding their doughnuts and coffee . . . bodies without brains, a pitiful sight.

One day I wandered down to the candy store, where we could buy soft drinks, combs, candy and other personal needs. I noticed a door at the side of the room, and out of curiosity more than anything else, I went over to it and turned the doorknob. To my surprise, it opened, and outside I could see a long stretch of green grass, with a street in the far distance. I stepped out.

Once on the grass, I took off running. I was finally outside those forbidding walls that stood high on my left. I stretched my legs to their fullest, for I felt I would never get away from those buildings, never get beyond the grass under my feet. I didn't slow down until the hospital was far behind me.

* * * *

My first step up on securing my freedom was to buy a six-pack of beer (using the money I'd planned to spend in the hospital candy shop), and then I took to the road. A friendly truck driver soon stopped, and after I'd settled in the seat beside him and found out where he was going, I offered him a beer, which he accepted. But when I leaned over to open the pull-top can for him, I felt the truck jerk so that it almost went careening off the highway. He had obviously gotten a look for the first time at the lettering on the back of my khaki shirt — "State Hospital South, Blackfoot."

"Hey, buddy — no sweat!" I told him. "I'm okay — you're okay. Just let me off at Caribou Creek . . . no problem!"

I had downed four of the six cans of beer by the time we got there, and the trucker swung off the road to take me directly to the Hastings house, where I walked up and knocked on the door.

Somewhere in the back of my mind was a vague idea that I could explain to them what had happened — why I'd taken the baby — and since they'd been helpful before, they'd be glad to help me again. When Betty answered the door, her hand went to her mouth, but I didn't wait. I just pushed open the door and went into the living room, where her mother was sitting on the divan.

"How — how are you, Gary?" The words were a forced whisper from Mrs. Hastings, and anyone could see they were both extremely frightened.

"Oh, fine — just fine," I said. "How's the baby?"

"Oh, he's fine, too!" Betty said quickly, too quickly.

"It's a nice day," I said, although I'd discovered it was sort of chilly outside, with me in my shirt sleeves. There was no answer. They just sat there and nodded nervously. Finally, figuring I had to say something, I came up with, "How have you been?"

They both started to answer at once, fluttery, but I didn't hear them. A loud, solid knocking at the front door where I'd entered demanded attention. Neither woman moved, so I got up and went to the door.

When I opened it, there stood the six-foot-three Sheriff in his ten-gallon hat, just like he had appeared at the trailer the morning after I'd taken the baby. As before, he had his shotgun ready in one hand and the cuffs with leg chains in the other.

"Have to ask you to come with me, Mr. Fisher," the Sheriff said. I couldn't have been at the Hastings house more than five minutes. That truck driver hadn't wasted any time at all.

Overnight, in the jail cell I'd occupied before, I took stock of my situation. Whatever progress, if any, I'd made at the

Blackfoot Hospital had gone down the drain. All those shock treatments — wasted! I'd have to start all over. Gary Fisher had blown it again! And I started to cry.

The next day, when I got back to Blackfoot, still in chains, I discovered the officials there took a dim view of their patients discharging themselves from custody. This time, I was assigned immediately to the "Y-Building" — their Y-2 Ward, where the really down-the-tube patients were kept.

If I'd thought I'd been on the outer perimeters of hell before, when I was in the open ward, I knew I'd descended into the pit of it now. The patients here were completely out of it, totally insane. I found a bed and lay down on it, and fatigue caught up with me, so I slept fitfully.

When I awoke, there were four big guys in coveralls standing over me, giggling and gesturing. I could imagine what they had in mind, so I jumped up and ran for the bathroom, but it was even worse in there. Three men were throwing their stool-contents at each other, while off to one side another one was masturbating himself while a second one closely watched. The stench turned my stomach, and I had no choice but to go back into the big room. It was unbelievable!

But what was the most frightening thing of all here — just as it had been in the other ward — was that no one seemed to do anything about the abnormal actions going on. The attendants seemed to ignore all the weird happenings, dismissing them as something to be expected. There was a big glass partition, and on one side were the women, while on the other side were the men. The staff people working there — doctors, nurses, orderlies, whatever — mostly just watched, doing nothing to stop the terrible things that went on.

When I went back into the big room again, I found all sorts of things in progress: one fellow was busy plowing an imaginary field; another thought he was George Washington, and wanted to tell everyone about it; while I watched, a sad little old lady just spread her legs and did her bathroom bit all over herself, then she screamed at the top of her lungs and started walking back and forth across what she'd done; one whining man threw a checkerboard at another because he hadn't won their game.

The smell alone was enough to blow my mind. Some sat by the wall, picking at themselves. Others chewed on their hands. The filth in the place was incredible . . . vomit . . . excrement . . . urine . . . it as as though these poor souls had been doomed to everlasting hell prematurely, and they were undergoing its torments while still living an earthly existence.

The nights were filled with screams, plus the terror of possible homosexual atrocity. I ended up getting my sleep during the day, sitting straight up with my back against the wall, for at night I dared not close my eyes. Many of the patients around me would stand up during most of the night, talking to themselves, occasionally screaming out as if in pain or terror, chattering of snakes and elephants and other fantasies. One muddled fellow made love to his wife — who wasn't there — all night long. And much of the time the poor souls looked like so many bombs getting ready to explode.

At mealtime, we'd be herded together into the mess hall, where the inmates would flip their heads back and laugh in demoniac fashion, throwing their food all over themselves, getting it into their ears, their hair, anywhere but where it belonged. I think if I'd had to take one more day — indeed, one more hour — of that association, I'd have joined them in complete mental degeneracy.

I began begging the psychiatrist to let me out of the Y-building, and after more days than I care to remember, he finally got down to business about it.

"You were placed there because you ran away, Gary," he said seriously. "I want to be sure you know that."

"Oh, man, do I know it!" I almost shouted. "Please, doctor, just let me out!"

"Will you promise not to run away again?"

"I promise! No way!" I meant it. In all my worst trips, I could never have imagined the living nightmare that I experienced in that advanced illness ward.

"All right," the doctor agreed. "You're out. I'll assign you back to the open ward." He grinned. "But watch your step!"

"Believe me, I will!" I promised. That night, I did join some of the young guys in that ward with another of their after-shave lotion drinking parties. Combined with my daily dose of pills, some of which I'd saved up for just such an occasion, it put me on a pretty good high — loaded enough so I could smile, but not so bombed that I could get in trouble — just enough to make the place endurable a little longer.

But it was not to be forever. I was sitting and watching the television in the ward a day or so later, when the doctor came in and sat down beside me. He said a couple of things about the ward and the weather, and then he dropped his lightning bolt: "Gary, we're releasing you today."

I jerked around to look at him. I couldn't believe my ears. He was kidding me. "Huh? What?" I couldn't put it together. "You mean . . . it's over?"

He smiled reassuringly. "That's right. We think we've done just about all we can for you."

I tried to think of proper words to express my gratitude. "Well, uh — thanks! I'll — be glad to get — away."

"We do have some serious advice for you, Gary," the doctor said then. "I hope you'll take it."

"Sure!" I vowed. "Whatever — you say."

"Stay off the drugs," the doctor said. "No more terpin hydrate, no pills of any kind. You're close to crystalizing your kidneys now. If you take that stuff much longer — or anything else, for that matter — it won't be long before you reach the point where your kidneys will stop functioning."

I nodded. He was laying out a large order for me.

"And that goes for booze, too," the doctor went on. "I guess you know you're an alcoholic."

I nodded. He wasn't sparing me anything.

"I know you've had a rough life," he continued. "but fortunately, you're still young enough to overcome all of it." He put his hand on my shoulder. "If you ever reach a point where you think you're ready for help — and I hope you do, the sooner the better — find a private psychiatrist and give him a chance to help straighten things out. It's the best thing you can do."

He stood up and extended his hand to me. "Now, let's go get you processed out of here. Good luck!"

I looked toward the window. Outside! I was going outside! I

was leaving this place! Tears sprang to my eyes, and I could hardly stand still long enough to go through the checking-out process.

But when I walked away from State Hospital South in Blackfoot, I became the same guy who'd entered it — how many weeks — months — had it been? I didn't know; it seemed like years. But no sooner had I put it behind me than the monkey crawled right up on my back again. I headed for a bar, got a drink, and then hit the road for Caribou Creek, the closest thing to being a hometown to me, and the only place that came to mind.

By late afternoon, I was drunk, but I'd found that elusive job I'd looked for there before. A service station on the highway needed a hand, and I was ready. I wasn't used to drinking, though, and the booze caught up to me. I got a bit loose, and late in the day, the Sheriff stopped by to give me a polite "Howdy-do," the only difference being that this time he wasn't holding a shotgun and chains.

"Reckon you'd like to go back to Blackfoot with me?" he said by way of welcome.

"Man!" I screamed. "Not that. Please don't take me back there!"

He pushed back the oversize hat and scratched his head. "All right," he said, "tell you what I'll do. I'll put you in jail overnight and give you a chance to dry out. Then, I'm going to get you a ticket on the train tomorrow morning, and if you'll take that train out of this town and never come back, we won't send you to Blackfoot!"

"All right!" I yelled. "Let's go!" So it was back to the little upstairs jail cell, the third time I'd pulled its latchstring.

And sure enough, next morning, the Sheriff brought a train ticket with him, and waited till I'd trod down the stairs to put the cuffs and leg irons on. Then he drove me to the train station. We sat there in his wagon — me in the back with all the steel mesh surrounding me — until the train came, and then he marched me with those mincing steps, the best I could make, up inside the passenger car. Only when I'd sat down in the seat did he take off the handcuffs, and unlock the chains from my legs.

There was quite a stir about that time. The people in the car, taking this all in, apparently decided they were being honored with the company of Pretty Boy Floyd or Machine Gun Kelly, so they got up en masse and moved to another part of the train.

"Got one thing to tell you," the Sheriff said, after he'd removed the irons. "This train ticket didn't come your way out of the goodness of my heart."

I stared at him, not knowing what he was getting at.

"The Hastings family — Mr. Hastings — paid for this ticket and added a little cash to give you one last chance to get away and make something of yourself," the Sheriff went on. "If I was you, it'd be a late day in August before I'd ever show up in these parts again. Good luck!" He handed me an envelope and was gone.

The train jerked into motion. I was leaving Idaho, probably forever. A new start. Someone cared enough to give me a chance to make something of myself. It was an exciting thought, but looming even bigger in my mind was the eternal craving for the drugs that would dim the problems that always dogged me. It was a burning sensation I could not ignore. At the first stop, I jumped off the train, went into a drugstore, and bought a couple of bottles of terpin hydrate with codeine, then picked up some lemons at a nearby grocery store before getting back on the train to Los Angeles.

The mental institution at Blackfoot was behind me. I truly had no idea how long I'd been there. In later years, I could look back and firmly believe it had been weeks, months, even a year or more. Only recently, when my personal doctor obtained my medical records from State Hospital South in Blackfoot, did I learn *I had spent only twenty-eight days there.*

With all I'd experienced and witnessed, it seemed like twenty-eight years!

Chapter Ten

How long I stayed in southern California following my release from Blackfoot in March, 1964, I am not sure, but I do know it didn't take very long for me to realize there was nothing for me there, and I took to the road again for Seattle . . . the familiar journey filled with heartache and frustration.

I don't know what I expected when I went to my mother's home in Seattle. I had no right to expect anything, of course, except rejection. And that's what I got.

"I'm sorry, Gary," she told me. "We just can't have you living here anymore; your stepfather won't stand still for it. You're all messed up," she went on, "and you refuse to do what's right. You're just going to have to go out and take care of yourself."

I'd been pushed out the door in the past, though never quite so firmly as this time.

"Okay, Mom," I told her. "Don't get all uptight. I'll go!"

Then she delivered the final blow. "And don't come back!" she said. But because she was my mother, at the same time she handed me a five-dollar bill. "That's the last time!" she said, and I turned away.

"Thanks, Mom," I murmured.

It didn't take long for the fiver to disappear, and for quite a time after that, I bummed around Seattle, living a hand-to-mouth existence based mostly on drugs. There was a standard routine I followed to get enough terpin hydrate to stay loaded on — a routine of hustling people.

It was still cold and blustery — sometimes snowing, often raining — in Seattle, and I used the weather to help me work my plan. I'd hitchhike here and there, and on stopping, I'd go to cocktail lounges, drugstores, gas stations, or even more frequently, to a bar. There, I'd ask the bartender if I could speak to the manager or the owner. I kept myself cleaned up, because it added to the plausibility of my act.

When the person in charge would come out, I'd have a set story. "I just moved into town," I'd say, "and I haven't found a job yet. I have a seven-year-old daughter at home who gets asthma attacks. She has a real bad cold now, and she's coughing pretty badly."

Then I'd sort of choke up myself. "Coughing brings on the asthma," I would say, hanging my head. "The doctor told me to pick up some medicine at the drugstore, but it costs a dollar and thirty-six cents, plus the tax."

I would look the man or woman straight in the eye at this point. "I need to make this money. I'm willing to work for it — I'll clean your bathrooms, sweep your floor, do your dishes, anything — if you'll just let me make this dollar thirty-six!"

Nine times out of ten, I didn't have to work. The person would usually hand me a five-dollar bill, and say, "Look, man, you go ahead and take this. Maybe sometime you'll run into someone else who's in trouble, and you can help them. See you later."

Of course it didn't always work out that way. Sometimes the people I'd hustle for cash would want to follow-up to make sure I was on the level. So they'd walk all the way to the drugstore with me, and go inside, where I'd buy the codeine cough medicine, as if I was really buying it for my daughter. Then I'd sign the book, a requirement with the purchase of narcotic drugs.

And then, the person with me might say, "Look, I'll give you a ride home — I know you're walking." I couldn't very well refuse, so it could turn out to be a pretty close shave, for they might want to walk right inside the house. Fortunately for me, I was again sharing Bill's pad at the time, so when we would get there, I'd jump out of the car quickly, tossing a "Thanks a lot, see you later!" over my shoulder, and I'd go into the house like I was anxious to get the medicine to my daughter.

That's how I worked for a long time. I could make anywhere from twenty to thirty dollars a day this way, and never get busted by the cops. But as time went on, I had to travel further and further, because the druggists wouldn't sell me the cough medicine more than once a week, and I had to be careful not to go back too often. And the more I drank the stuff, the more it took to get me high, finally reaching the point where I was drinking four bottles of terpin hydrate a day. That meant four different drugstores every day, and there are only so many drugstores in an area.

In White Center there were lots of taverns, but only three drugstores, so I had to range far and wide from there. It got so I'd have to go to at least seven different towns in a week so I could get my drugs, and that meant traveling from fifty to sixty miles a day.

The pharmacists weren't stupid, and some of them got to know me well enough they cut me off, realizing someone had to be using the stuff much more than he should. So I'd have to travel still further, always with the thumb out. It was, to say the least, a bummer.

Often, it was hard to catch a ride. I'd get soaking wet in the rain, and that would blow my high, and I'd finally get home and swear to myself that I was going to get off this stuff . . . I would kick my worthless habit. So I'd lie in bed all day, and around five o'clock I'd get sick from withdrawal, then I'd panic because I knew the drugstores would close at nine o'clock. So I'd hit the road again, looking for a drugstore where I could get more terpin hydrate without a hassle.

More than once I decided I'd switch to booze to get off the codeine kick, totally ignoring the advice of the doctor who'd signed me out at Blackfoot. I recall once when I decided that was the best way to go, I bought a couple of fifths of whiskey and drank both of them, but I didn't get high. I just got deathly sick, so sick I couldn't get out of bed.

Out of my past came the knowledge that this was a matter for Alcoholics Anonymous to handle, so I called them, and then held a butcher knife at my stomach, wishing I had the guts to push it in so I could die before someone came to help me out. But I couldn't do it, and the man who came from AA — even though he tried hard — didn't do me much good, either.

Another time, I met a sympathetic girl who — like the one in Idaho — wanted to help, so she took me to her home. Her mother, however, must have had every kind of pills you could think of in her medicine cabinet — muscle relaxers, sleeping pills, tranquilizers, I don't know what all. So I took a few out of each bottle, and started taking them little by little. The result just about blew my mind — I ended up lying on their front room floor, talking gibberish. I couldn't get myself together at all, and finally the girl's mother realized what I'd done.

"I never heard of such a thing!" she gasped. But the next day was Sunday, and she sincerely wanted to aid a down-and-outer.

"If you'll go to church with us tomorrow, we'll try to help you," she told me, and I could only nod. I couldn't trust my tongue to say the right words at that point.

So I went to church with them the next day, but I sat in the back, and when no one was looking, I slipped out and went to a nearby drugstore and bought a bottle of terpin hydrate. On the way home they could smell the stuff on me, and that was all it took.

"Out! On your way! We just can't have this kind of thing!" She was one displeased lady, and I couldn't really blame her, so I split. But I still had some of those assorted pills in my pocket, and when I got to Bill's place, I downed them all.

The resulting "trip" was something else. My mind simply snapped with the pressures of those mixed medications, and I couldn't remember where I was. I couldn't form any words no matter how hard I tried, and around me, the chairs started turning into people. For the next three days I couldn't carry on a conversation. Thinking back to my days at Blackfoot, I was frightened beyond belief. Was I destined to return to the snake-pit? I had to do something!

My solution wasn't exactly what a doctor would have ordered. I decided the only way I could get off my drug kick was to kill it with booze. Not only that, I decided I needed another change of scene, so I went down to Seattle's skid row, rented myself a room for a dollar a week, and got a jug of wine. You can't really imagine what it was like . . . the place was absolutely filthy — men and women lying in the hallways, cockroaches and lice all over, the dregs of society, at the bottom of an endless hellhole.

This was indeed a sort of repetition of what I'd experienced at Blackfoot, except there was less than no help for anyone here. I'd lie in that rotten room and stare at the tiny light over the sink, afraid to turn it off for fear someone would shoot me or stab me or try to take away what little money I had left. The only good that existed for any of us there was an undefined sense of brotherhood — the code of the streets — wherein a bunch of us would get together in the front room of the hotel, pooling our dimes and nickels in a hat so there'd be enough to buy a bottle of wine for all to share and share alike.

Upstairs, a wino Indian woman would sell her body to get more alcohol, and she was constantly asking for nickels and dimes. Again paralleling the Idaho mental institution, a bunch of us would sit in her room while she was having sex with someone else, drinking wine and paying no attention to the crazy acts going on. But it didn't bother us, for we were in a world of our own — a world of hell, without the fire.

There came a day when, stoned as usual, I walked into the second floor living room of the hotel, sat down on a couch, and began talking with a Black — a small man, who had become a good friend. About that time a big Indian came in, and for no reason at all, started hassling my friend. Loaded as I was, I took offense at his action, and jumped up and grabbed the Indian by the shoulders. I intended to push him up against the wall, but in my drunken fury I missed the wall and shoved him right through a window. How I had managed to manhandle that huge Indian, I'll never know.

When the window shattered, I cut both my arms. I was back on the couch trying to stop the bleeding when the Indian climbed back through the window, grabbed me by the throat, and crashed his big fist into my face, knocking two front teeth loose.

He was wearing a heavy overcoat, and when I pushed him

Among good childhood memories were weekends when Gary's father would pick up Gary (right), and his brother, Earl (Bud), for brief fun periods away from the supervised home for troubled and abused boys where they lived.

Seldom a "winner," Gary did capture a Soapbox Derby trophy with his entry. Here, a representative of the sponsoring Chevrolet garage shares the triumph with Gary.

Sneaking a "shot" of available alcoholic mixtures from a bottle at a remote spot on the schoolground was a typical action in Gary's high school years.

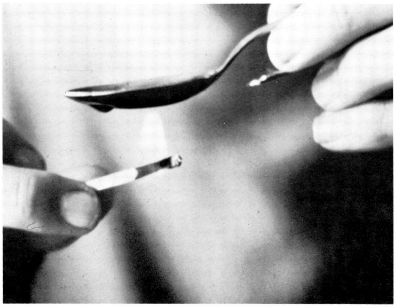

Gary's ultimate drug abuse — hard drugs via the needle — is illustrated here in the "cooking" process, preparatory to an injection of heroin.

"When . . . when . . . when . . . will I ever be free from being locked up?" Gary's face behind a fence shows his continuing frustration with his self-induced plight in life.

The basement where Gary descended to the pits of emotional disturbance — an attempt to kill his mother — illustrates the desperation of his predicament, before light finally dawned in his life.

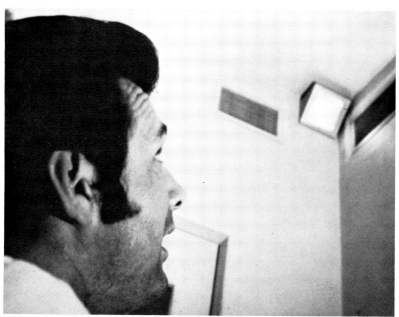

Desperation of the padded cell is unnerving at best — another experience that Gary repeated time and again in his continuing search for the reality of life.

The frustration of being strapped down in a mental institution (a frequent experience for Gary) is reflected here.

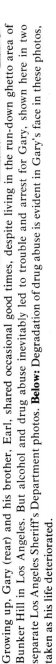

Growing up. Gary (rear) and his brother, Earl, shared occasional good times, despite living in the run-down ghetto area of Bunker Hill in Los Angeles. But alcohol and drug abuse inevitably led to trouble and arrest for Gary, shown here in two separate Los Angeles Sheriff's Department photos. **Below:** Degradation of drug abuse is evident in Gary's face in these photos, taken as his life deteriorated.

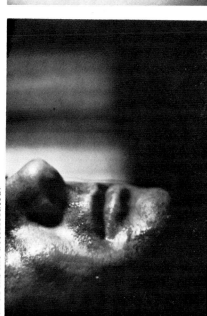

A typical scene in an auditorium shows Gary presenting his incredible account of an abused life turned completely around after making a decision for Christ.

As Chaplain of the Solid Rock Coffee House in Sylmar (a Los Angeles suburb), Gary (center), prepares for baptismal services in a San Gabriel Mountains' stream.

Gary (right), shows his first book, *Satan's Been Cross Since Calvary,* to his brother, Bud — Dr. Earl Fisher, U.S. Navy. The book contains a series of Gary's successful sermons using nursery rhymes, fairy tales and familiar Bible stories as themes.

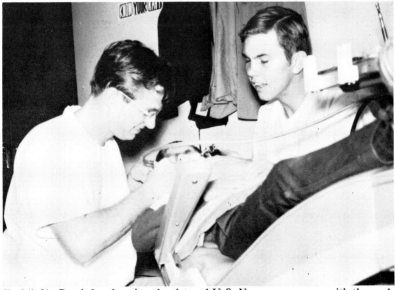

Earl (left), Gary's brother, is a dentist and U.S. Navy career man, with the rank of Lieutenant Commander.

Wedding day for Gary and Nanell was, in Gary's words, "the most exciting time in my life, other than making a decision for Christ." Nanell is an ex-drug abuser who joined Gary in presenting "Dope Stop" seminars to high school and college students.

The love of a Christian home is shared not only by Gary and Nanell, but also their son, Shane, whose arrival on December 23, 1971, was the answer to their prayers. Today they have two other formerly abused children whom they've adopted.

out the window he landed on the second story fire escape. Now, he was choking me, and I was sure this was it . . . I was about to die. My whole useless life flashed through my mind, and I had a fleeting thought that perhaps it was just as well.

The Indian was screaming at the top of his lungs. "Nobody pushes me out a window!" he shrilled, clamping those monstrous fingers around my throat.

But when he'd tumbled out of the window, patrolmen on the street below had seen him and they came running upstairs, grabbed the Indian, and pulled him off of me. The familiar handcuffs were snapped on both of us and we rode to jail in the paddy wagon, went through the booking process, and ended up in the same cell.

"Hey, man, I'm sorry I got you into this," I said to the big Indian after the iron door clicked shut. "I guess I just went crazy, out of my mind with that cheap wine — you know what I mean?"

"Sure," he said, "that's okay. I started bugging that other guy, anyway. No hard feelings." And he held out his ham-sized hand for me to shake.

We talked some more, and soon discovered we had a lot in common, chiefly our problems with drugs and alcohol, and the sordid life on Seattle's skid row. And a little later, when we both went before a judge — me being booked on attempted manslaughter — my new friend had a ready answer when asked if he wished to press charges.

"Naw," he said. "That was all a mistake. My friend, here, he tripped and pushed me toward the window trying to keep his balance. Then I lost my balance, and I fell out the window." He looked toward me for confirmation. "It was just an accident."

I nodded my head while the judge consulted his papers and then looked down at both of us over his glasses. "Five days in jail for both of you for drunkenness," he announced.

I served this time, hardly conscious of the passing hours, because the familiar pains of withdrawal racked my tired body day and night. When it was over I went back to the streets, hustling some cash with my asthma-prone daughter story so I could get my head twisted — and get rid of the torment gnawing at my vitals. I managed to get a bottle of terpin hydrate, along with a couple of beers, so I was coasting again, and I returned to the cheap hotel, to lie down in my sleazy room.

For a while, I counted the spiders in the corners, and made images out of the dirt splotches that were all over the place. I could hear people yelling and cursing in the hallway outside my room. When I had to go to the bathroom down the hall, I was scared half to death that someone would come in and rip my pants or shoes off.

I got up hungry the next morning, and bought a bowl of soup for ten cents at a small cafe across the street. It was the best I could do. And before the day had worn into its later hours, I managed to hitch a ride to another part of town, where I talked my way into enough cash to buy another bottle of terpin hydrate, along with a bottle of muscatel wine. By this time, I didn't care what I mixed. Anything to get loaded — that was my motto, and I practiced it daily.

I had the two bottles with me, but it was cold and raining steadily outside and I was far from my gimcrack hotel room, so I decided to take advantage of the first available roof I could put over my head. It didn't bother me at all that it was a large building with a cross above it. All that mattered was that its front door opened when I pushed on it, and inside it was dry and quiet and there were plenty of places for me to sit down. I proceeded to choke down the cough medicine, and then drank a sizable portion of the muscatel.

What happened then, I can only reconstruct from what has been told to me. Apparently, the combination of wine and codeine was too potent for me to handle; I blacked out and lay there until sometime later when the priest came upon my inert body. Checking me for identification, he found my mother's telephone number, called her, and asked her to come and get me. And once again compassion overcame her good judgment and she drove to the church to pick me up.

My first vague memory of the incident was coming to, glancing around to see where I was, and upon finding my mother at the wheel of the car, opening the door and jumping out to roll across the street into the gutter. Behind us, a man slammed on the brakes of his car, got out, came over and picked me up, and dragged me back to my mother's auto. I felt like I'd been run over by a truck; I must have looked like I'd just gone fifteen rounds with Rocky Marciano at his prime.

Of the remainder of the ride home, I have no recall. Once there, my mother helped me stumble into the basement, but when she'd led me to the bed and turned to go, I suddenly suspected she intended to lock me inside because she was afraid of me, and I flipped. Again, I have no remembrance of what happened — I only know what others told me, for I blacked out completely.

I woke up the next morning on the couch in the living room to see my stepfather slowly coming down the stairs. "Do you know you tried to strangle your mother yesterday?" he said quietly.

I shook my head, trying to clear it. "No way!" I said. "I'd never do a thing like that!"

He frowned grimly. "You never will admit you're all the way to the bottom, will you, Gary?"

I knew he was lying. Without a word, I got up from the couch and swung up the stairs three at a time to my mother's bedroom. And there was my mother, with a fear in her eyes I'd never seen before. She turned her face to the wall and I saw black-and-blue marks all over her throat.

Slowly, I went back down the stairs, got my coat, a change of clothes, and an old suitcase, and left the house. For once I didn't have to be asked to leave. I had finally reached the ultimate in abuse — I had tried to kill my own mother!

Dragging my feet down the sidewalk, I tried to get a hold of myself. I felt like some kind of monster. I didn't know which way to turn. The old craving for codeine was a dingy taste in my mouth. I knew, without thinking about it, that I'd be on the trail of more terpin hydrate before many hours had passed. Yet, I knew I couldn't face the degradation of skid row again, not for a while, at least. So I headed for a place I thought perhaps would offer refuge — the little house where my friend, Bill, lived.

"Sure, Gary," he said in his usual casual fashion. "You can hang your hat here anytime — you know that! Just make yourself at home."

I was grateful to him — so grateful I went inside, found the spare bed I'd used before, and lay down. Bill was leaving as I arrived, so I was solitary again with the one almost constant companion I'd learned to live with — loneliness.

I lay on the bed with tears coursing down my cheeks; after twenty-six and a half years, I had finally reached bottom.

Chapter Eleven

I had reached the absolute end of the line, and I knew it. I thought of the days and nights I'd spent on Seattle's Jackson Street, usually with no money in my pockets. I thought about the unwanted strays who wandered around there — not dogs, people. Many were young, many had come from good homes, many had become homosexuals. I had seen some pitiful sights, and I had become a pitiful sight myself.

How long I stayed there crying softly to myself, I have no idea, but sometime that afternoon, I left Bill's house and headed for nearby Rat City (White Center), intent only on getting enough drugs or booze or both to get loaded. But before I could get hold of either, a young fellow — about sixteen — pushed a small piece of paper into my hand as I walked past him on the street. I'd seen kids like him before, but I'd never paid much attention to what they were distributing. As far as I was concerned everyone was pushing something . . . and if these kids wanted to pass out little leaflets, let them do their thing.

Only this time, for some reason I was curious about the whole thing, so I walked into the closest bar. "My eyes are kind of out of focus," I said to the bartender. "Can you tell me what this says?" and I pointed to the large print across the top of the little piece of paper.

He squinted at it in the dim light. " 'The Positive Cure for a Drug Addict,' " he read. Then, after glancing over the smaller print, he looked up. "It's one of those religious things. Claims you can cure addicts with religion — you know, Jesus Christ!"

I nodded. But those first words, "The Positive Cure for a Drug Addict," had somehow hit me where it hurt. I was not inclined to believe them, whatever they had to offer, but if there was a cure for drug addiction, I was certainly interested in finding out what it was.

"Put out by Teen Challenge, Chicago, Illinois," the bartender seemed to be reading as much to himself as to me. Then he glanced at me. "Ever hear of Dave Wilkerson? He started this thing. How about Nicky Cruz . . . Sonny Arguinzoni?"

I didn't want to admit anything, so I shook my head. "They're all mixed up in it," the bartender said, handing the tract back to me. "What'll you have?"

"Oh — nothing right now — I'll be back," I said. "Thanks for — reading that for me." I edged toward the door. The stuff on that little sheet of paper had suddenly become very important to me, so much so I was actually ready to ignore what I'd come to Rat City for. Outside, I turned back the way I'd come, figuring I could get Bill to read the rest of the paper to me.

I'd heard those names all right — on the streets, in the missions — but I'd never paid much attention to them. These were just some guys with a different kind of racket, the way I figured it. But a positive cure for a drug addict — now that was something else! If ever anyone was looking for that, it was me. I got back to the house and stretched out on my bed again, waiting for Bill to come back from work so he could fill me in on this cure business.

But Bill didn't come home, so I dug the piece of paper out of my pocket again, and began trying to figure it out for myself. I recognized the name *Jesus Christ* again and again, and I gathered that guys like Nicky and Sonny had been introduced to Jesus by Dave Wilkerson, who, according to the bartender, was apparently at a place called Teen Challenge in Chicago, Illinois. That was enough for me. I packed my suitcase and went out to stand on the street corner, waiting for a ride. I would go to Chicago myself to find Dave Wilkerson, and then he could turn me on to Jesus Christ, and I'd no longer be a dope addict. It was the first hope I'd found in months . . . even years!

I'd always been fairly lucky at hitching rides, but with an old overcoat on to protect me against the mixed rain and snow on that Seattle street corner, and with the way I must have looked, there was no way anyone was going to pick me up. My two front teeth were gone, my continuing drug habit had left me skinny and frail and I probably looked like I was sixty years old. So I waited and waited, and no one would stop, and finally I had to give it up. No one was going to take me to Illinois where I could get help from Dave Wilkerson and this Teen Challenge the leaflet told about.

I dragged myself through the sodden chill of the night, back to Bill's empty house, and as if I hadn't become wet enough sloshing through the rain and snow, the tears began to flow again. I lay there and wept, because I knew there wasn't any way I could find the help I needed so desperately.

I hadn't picked up any drugs or any booze that night, and though the pains were beginning to push me, I had made up my mind I wasn't going to take anything again. So I decided there was only one thing to do. I'd spent a lot of time in the pokey, and since I couldn't get to Chicago, maybe the best answer was to have myself locked up. Then, at least, I wouldn't have any access to pills or wine or any of the other combinations I'd abused my body with. If it was a choice of Jesus or jail — and if Jesus was a couple of thousand miles away at a place called Teen Challenge — then I'd have to settle for jail. I reached for Bill's telephone and asked the operator for the police station.

"Police Department — Sergeant Smith."

"Hey, can you came get me and put me away?" I blurted. "I need to be locked up!"

"Yeah?" Sergeant Smith said, with a sort of tolerant kindness in his voice. "What seems to be the problem?"

"I'm a pillhead!" I told him. "I got a real bad habit, and my stomach's inside out. I'm tired of trying to fight it, and I figure if I can't hack it alone, maybe you guys —"

"What's your name, buddy?"

I was afraid to give it to him right. "Gary," I said, "Gary Kearney," using one of the phony names which I'd often signed when picking up narcotic cough medicine at drugstores.

"Gary," Sergeant Smith said then, still in the same friendly,

personal tone, "we could lock you up all right, but I don't think
that would solve anything. You need help, and getting locked up
won't give you that help."

"But I got to do something! I'm desperate!" I told him.

"All right, listen, I have a suggestion," the sergeant went
on, like he'd been waiting to see just how serious I was.
"There's a new organization here in Seattle called Teen Challenge. They're doing a lot of good work with dopers and boozers.
I think they might be what you're looking for."

"*You got to be kidding!*" I yelled.

"No," came the patient answer. "I was never more
serious."

"No, what I mean is," I managed to say, "I was trying to get
to Teen Challenge earlier tonight. I didn't know they had one
here in Seattle. Boy!"

"I've got their number right here, Gary," Sergeant Smith
said. "You want to take it down?"

"Do I!" I said. "Hang on a minute — let me get a pencil!"

In my usual laborious fashion, I took the number, thanked
Sergeant Smith for his help, and started to hang up the phone.

"Talk to a man named Larry Hillis," were the policeman's
parting words. "He'll do all he can to help. And — good luck,
Gary!"

Teen Challenge . . . right there in Seattle! I dialed the
number, suddenly realizing that it might be too late to reach
anyone — it was three o'clock in the morning!

As I listened to the buzz of the phone ringing, out of the
night panic struck again! *Teen Challenge* — I was far past the
teenage years. Did that mean I wasn't eligible? The thought
came to me, hang up before anyone answers, but just then, a
voice came on the telephone.

"Teen Challenge for Christ — this is Larry Hillis."

A warm, friendly voice, despite the hour. "This is Gary
Fisher," I said, spilling out my real name before I realized it. "I
— I was told you might be able to — help me."

"Gary — if you have a problem, and you must have or you
wouldn't have called — we'll do whatever we can."

"I — I'm not a teenager," I explained. "I —"

The firm, confident voice interrupted. "Would you like to come down to the Teen Challenge Center, and we can talk about it?"

"Yeah," I said, hopefully. "I sure would."

"We'll come and get you right now," Larry Hillis told me. "Where are you, Gary?"

I gave him the address, heard him say, "We'll be there in twenty minutes," and then add, "Just hang on till we get there, Gary." I promised that I would.

While I was waiting, I looked in the refrigerator and in all of the cupboards to see if I could find some beer or maybe some terpin hydrate I'd misplaced, so I could fortify myself for the coming encounter with Teen Challenge, whatever it would be. But I was out of luck. There wasn't a drop of anything, not even a pill, in sight. I'd cleaned them all out. So I sat by my packed suitcase and shakily smoked one cigarette after another.

I was startled when the knock came on the door. What was I getting into? I wondered. Would Dave Wilkerson, the man I'd started out to find that night, be at the Teen Challenge Center in Seattle? Was Jesus Christ there? I was frightened, an experience I'd gone through many times before. But I was also desperate. I opened the door.

"Hi, Gary!" The broad smile on the face of the handsome young man who stood there was matched with a friendly hand extended to me. I stuck out my own hand and winced at the firm squeeze it got. "I'm Larry Hillis. All set?"

I nodded. "Got to get my suitcase," I said, turning back into the room.

But Larry moved past me toward the couch. "Here, I'll carry that." It was the first time I could remember anyone I didn't know being so free to offer me an assist.

I turned out the light, set the lock on the door, and followed the Teen Challenge man to a blue stationwagon parked at the curb, where I found another surprise.

"Gary, I want you to meet our Harvester's Trio," Larry said, and I saw three pretty girls sitting in the back. "This is Linda, that's Becky, and the tall one is Trina. Girls, this is Gary."

They all said, "Hi, Gary!" and the auto started in motion.

"Gary, did you know Jesus loves you?" I didn't know which girl asked the question, and I didn't know the answer, so I just nodded and kept looking straight ahead. But I was touched by the vibrant atmosphere in that car; I'd never seen anyone so exuberantly happy, bubbling over with enthusiasm. It felt like stepping into a bottle of something clean.

"You can win every battle, you can climb every mountain with Jesus Christ at your side." A different voice, but the same genuine sincerity. I nodded again, afraid to look around. I still wasn't sure what I'd gotten myself into, but so far it gave me a good, hopeful feeling.

"We'll pray for you, Gary!" A third voice. "You'll pray, too, won't you?"

I'd heard lots of praying when I'd visited the missions on Seattle's skid row and at street corner meetings with the Salvation Army, but I didn't see how that was going to help me break my drug habit. However, I nodded anyway, and nervously reached for a cigarette.

"Have to ask you not to smoke, Gary," Larry Hillis said quietly. "One of our Teen Challenge disciplines."

Quickly — embarrassed — I shoved the cigarette back into the pack. No smoking? What kind of a deal was this? Was I getting into some weird kind of jail? I fidgeted while the girls chattered on among themselves until the stationwagon finally stopped, and I saw that we'd come to a good-sized three-story building, with a broad expanse of lawn around it.

There was a prayer meeting of some sort going on in a big front room when we went inside, and before I knew it, someone was praying for me. I wasn't sure what good this would do, but remembering my days back at Blackfoot, I decided that the best thing to do was "get into the program." I would give Teen Challenge a try. It just might work!

"Gary," Larry Hillis said to me after the prayer was finished, "the Lord wants to help you with your problems. All you have to do is ask Jesus Christ to come into your life, and you'll be born again. Are you ready?"

"Yeah, I guess so."

"When you confess with your mouth and believe in your

heart that Jesus was resurrected from the dead, you can be saved. Do you believe, Gary?''

"Sure," I said, wanting to be agreeable. "I believe."

"Praise God!" He put his hand on my shoulder. "Ask Jesus to come into your heart, Gary."

I figured it wouldn't hurt to give it a try. "Jesus, come into my heart," I mumbled. But I didn't feel anything. There was no explosion. I just felt tired. It was almost four o'clock in the morning. I wasn't sure what this was all about, and I didn't much care.

"Amen!"

That seemed to dismiss the meeting, and they led me to a small, dormitory-type room where I was glad to stretch out. The pains were with me again. Regulations or not, I smoked a cigarette before I went to sleep.

* * * *

Teen Challenge, I found, was based not only on a rigid personal discipline with a strict religious foundation, but it also involved keeping busy at productive activity. The operating philosophy apparently was to keep a drug addict so busy he didn't have time to think about drugs. And it worked!

First thing in the morning, before breakfast, there was a half-hour prayer meeting, on our knees — probably twenty of us, praying aloud by turns. Then a nourishing breakfast — something I wasn't used to — followed by clean-up time, and then a chapel service lasting till noon . . . songs, sermons, testimony. Lunch came at noon sharp, and after maybe a half-hour to rest and relax, we'd go out to witness for Christ on the street, or else stay at the Center for several hours of intensive Bible study.

We'd have dinner about five, do the kitchen cleanup detail again, and then get ourselves in shape for the evening's activities. Sometimes we went to church — a different one each night — to sing and give testimony. Or, if we had no church scheduled, we'd witness on the streets to the saving power of Jesus Christ. And if the routine of working for the Lord left any gaps, there was a mop or a broom or a rake or a lawnmower thrust into our hands. There was constant movement — no time to think of anything but what we were totally involved in — so that by bedtime we were ready to flop.

For the first time in many years, I felt that someone was sincerely interested in me, but beyond that, I didn't really feel much of a change in my life. I was willing to play along with these people, but I wasn't sure I was ready for the all-out dedication to Jesus Christ that they seemed to expect. I figured I could get by, by sitting on the fence, playing both sides. So I kept on smoking, even if it was against the rules.

I'd get up early in the morning before anyone else was awake, to go snipe hunting. That meant searching for roaches — cigarette butts — discarded by others, smoking what was left, and then sneaking back into the Center to wash my hands and put on some after-shave lotion in hopes I wouldn't be caught. I wasn't alone, of course — it was a technique used by a lot of guys who had the same trouble I did trying to give up smoking.

The problem was, the Teen Challenge staff had an uncanny sense of smell. They'd always sniff out that tobacco odor on our clothes and they'd come down on us hard — for discipline, which is tough love, was one of the things that made the Center so effective. To circumvent their regulations, I would go up to the top floor of the three-story building, climb through a high window up there, and get on the roof, where I could hide behind the chimney and smoke. I'd take after-shave lotion to wash my hands, and I'd sprinkle it on my clothes, but I didn't get away with it very long.

I came home from church one day and Nicky Cruz — one of Dave Wilkerson's original street gang converts who'd been mentioned in the pamphlet — called me into the office. "You're trying to play games with us, Gary," Nicky said seriously. "And it won't work."

He was right; I couldn't deny it, so I just stood there and looked at him like a kid caught with his hand in the cookie jar.

"When we say 'No Smoking,' we mean it!" Nicky went on. "And that means you, the same as everyone else!"

I nodded, still not saying anything. "You don't have to talk to me," Nicky said then, "but you do have to talk to God. Now get up to your room and pray — pray for strength. It's the only way you'll ever make it!"

I hadn't really learned how to pray yet, but I went to my room and made a half-hearted try at it. I hadn't been there five minutes before Nicky came bursting in.

"Give me your cigarettes, Gary!"

I was a little afraid of Nicky Cruz, who'd had a reputation as one of the toughest guys in all the New York street gangs. His voice of authority wouldn't be denied, so I dug my pack of cigarettes out from under the mattress where I'd hidden it in the bed springs, and gave him the smokes.

Nicky just dumped the whole pack out on the floor, and began stamping up and down on them. "Now," he said to me, "you're free! Thank you, Jesus!" By the time he was through tramping on them, my cigarettes looked like they were part of the floor.

I had to remind myself from time to time that I'd been ready to go as far away as Chicago, to find Dave Wilkerson and Teen Challenge. Although Dave wasn't there in Seattle, his program was. Everyone there did all they could to bring me to Jesus Christ, and on the surface, I played along with them; underneath, though, my heart wasn't in it. I was just marking time. And though I'd kicked my drug habit again, for the time being — and I really wanted to get rid of it so I could lead a normal life — I wasn't ready yet to accept the saving power of Jesus.

Perhaps to let me know I had reached a point where they felt they could trust me, and to give me a sense of responsibility, the Seattle Teen Challenge officials sent me to counsel one of their backsliders. Jack was a real cool guy. He drove a big Cadillac, and he had money to spend, and that was the kind of thing I could enjoy.

We were driving around the third day I was with him, and he said, "Gary, I'd like to show you something."

"Fine," I said, not knowing what he had in mind.

So we drove back to his home, where we went into his garage, and he pulled out a small box from its hiding place on a shelf. The minute I saw its contents, I knew what was up, though I'd never had any personal experience with such things.

The box held an "outfit" — a tiny syringe about like an eye dropper; a "spike" — the needle to attach to it; a short length of flexible rubber hose; a blackened teaspoon; and a small bottle of water.

"This will righteously give you a charge you wouldn't believe!" Jack explained to me as he emptied some white powder into the spoon from a little packet he carried. Then he poured a few drops of water on the powder, lit a match and held it under the spoon, and waited until the mixture began bubbling from the heat. Then he drew the solution into the syringe, and attached the needle. Moments later, he had tied the hose around his upper arm, and had "fixed" by injecting the stuff into his vein.

"How about it, Gary?" Jack turned to me with that engaging grin of his. "Want to go on a real trip?"

Already a drug addict, I had no resistance. This was something new, but if it would turn me on like Jack said, why not try it once? I'd never let it really get hold of me; after all, I could go back to Teen Challenge any time I wanted. So I didn't hesitate.

"Sure," I said. "Let's get it on!"

The white powder, Jack told me, was mojo — morphine. Within seconds after Jack stuck his needle into the vein at the point where forearm and upper arm join at the elbow, I felt a vibration that shook my entire body. There was a flash that knocked me to my knees. I wasn't sure what hit me, and I suddenly felt I was floating free of everything. It was a sensation never before equalled in all my years of drug addiction.

I continued to run with Jack, and I continued to turn on with morphine. I got my own outfit and spike, but I stayed on at Teen Challenge, still trying to play both sides of the fence, until it became apparent that everyone saw right through me. They knew I was jiving them, playing games, and it didn't go over. So more and more I began spending my time with Jack, shooting morphine and occasionally heroin, and the first thing I knew, Teen Challenge was simply another memory for me. I went back to Bill's pad, where I'd gone so many times before, but this time

I followed the hard drug crowd, a route I'd never been on previously. I played on poor Bill's sympathies to get the cash I needed to support my enlarged habit.

Unlike the typical heroin addict, I would fix all up and down my arms, not in just one spot. Before I was through, I must have had two or three hundred holes in my arms, clear down to the skin between my fingers.

A gram of morphine, available on the street from drugstore robberies that were a frequent occurrence, cost twenty dollars, and I recall a day when I was holding two grams at a party, and I decided to take off. But frightened as usual, I was fearful that with the morphine in my hand, I'd have to swallow it if I got stopped. So I called a taxi, and when I got to Bill's place, I didn't waste any time. I went to the bathroom and began getting ready to fix.

After I'd cooked my morphine in the spoon, I dropped my spike — the only one I had — and bent the end of it. I didn't have any tools to straighten the needle, so like the fool that I was, I took some sandpaper and started sanding the point. When I got through, it looked like an eight-penny nail. So when I tried to cram it into my vein, I had to push and push, but when I finally made it, the morphine simply bubbled up in the vein in a sort of clot, so I had to try it again.

I took the second gram and heated it up, and shot it into the other arm. And that one also bubbled up. I had missed getting loaded, because the stuff didn't go into my system. I'd wasted forty dollars worth of drugs, and they hadn't touched me. I sat down in a rocking chair, rocking back and forth and moaning to myself about my troubles when all of a sudden, the bubbles in both arm veins cut loose, and the morphine spread and hit my heart.

That did it! I knew I had over-dosed — there was no way my poor body could stand that much shock at once! I couldn't hold myself together, for I began to gray out, and I knew if I let myself go unconscious, I'd be a goner for sure.

I jumped up, running back and forth in the room and yelling. "Bill! Bill! Get an ambulance — I'm going out!" Bill, who'd been in another part of the house, came running in.

"Ambulance!" I repeated. "I'm O-D-ing!" I was flapping my arms back and forth like a chicken to keep my heart from stopping, because I knew I'd had too much.

Bill didn't waste any time; he called an ambulance service immediately, but by the time they got there, I'd decided I didn't want to go. There'd be too many questions about those holes in my arms. So the ambulance crew left, and then I felt the same sensation — blackout — again. But this time, I didn't ask Bill to call for help. I just hung in there all night, shuffling back and forth across the room, and about seven o'clock the next morning, weak and shaken, I walked to the hospital by myself. I worked up enough courage to go inside, but once there, I couldn't make myself ask to see a doctor. I just walked out and dragged myself back to the house. I could easily have died from using the needle; it's a wonder I didn't.

A while later, I found myself at a party where there was a lot of drinking and smoking grass (marijuana). In typical fashion, it looked like everyone was having a great time, but every time there was a knock on the door, or the telephone would ring, there was obvious dread carved in the faces around me.

Sitting there trying to be part of the scene, I noticed an ice pick on the coffee table, and it occurred to me if I didn't take that ice pick and hide it, someone might get mad and stab someone else, and then there would be trouble. So when I was sure no one was looking, I reached over and took the ice pick and stuck it inside my shoe. I waited a while, drank some more, and then decided I needed more drugs — I'd picked up some amps (amphetamines).

I found the bathroom, downed the pills, and with all the booze I'd already consumed, began to feel the giddiness that was typical when I was totally stoned. I turned out the light and opened the door to rejoin the rest of the party-goers, and in the darkness, a black figure loomed up in front of me. Without warning, he thrust himself at me, and I felt something jam into my side.

I thought I must have been hit with a broken beer bottle, for it felt like I'd been stabbed seven times with that one blow. I went down to the floor, screaming in pain. Then, heightening the already intense torment almost beyond endurance, my attacker pulled whatever he used out of my side. It felt like my entire insides were being pulled out, too.

Then he turned on the light. "Oh my God, Gary! I'm sorry, man!" His voice was anguished. "I thought you were going to stab me with that ice pick, and I had to get you first!"

It was one of the guys who'd been at the party when I got there, a fellow called Ace. Through pain-wracked eyes, I just lay there on the floor and looked up at him, my hand turning moist where I held it at my bleeding side.

"Look, man," Ace whispered hoarsely, "if you won't tell the fuzz, I'll take you down and buy you a hamburger. Don't cop out on me, Gary! Please!"

He grabbed a towel and tossed it to me, and I jammed it against the hole in my side. I sat up slowly, then managed to get to my feet. On the counter of the bathroom sink lay a pair of dirty, bloody shears — the kind used for heavy cutting. Ace had plunged them into me handle deep.

I leaned against the wall for a minute or so, trying to compose myself. The drugs I'd already had lessened the pain, and I didn't much care whether the cops came after Ace or not, so I wrapped the towel around me and followed him out of the house, where we got in his car and went to a nearby drive-in for a hamburger, just as he promised. The gash in my side didn't look as big now, so I figured I wasn't hurt too badly.

"Thanks for the burger," I told Ace after we'd eaten. "I'm going home."

So with the towel wrapped around me, I hitched a ride home, walked in on Bill, and loosened the bloody towel.

"Wow!" Bill said. "What happened to you?"

"Oh, I got stabbed a little bit," I told him. "Doesn't hurt now. I'll be okay."

He followed me to the bathroom, where I washed off the dried blood and looked at the inch-wide hole in my side. I felt sort of weak by now, so I went and laid down on the bed.

"You sure you're all right, Gary?" Bill was concerned. "Sure you don't want me to call a doctor — or take you to emergency?"

"Yeah," I assured him. "I'm all right. It'll heal up by morning."

So Bill went on to work the next day, and I slept until around eleven o'clock. When I stumbled out of bed to go to the bathroom — Shock!

My stomach was bloated beyond belief — so distended I looked like a seven-months pregnant woman. I realized vaguely, without really knowing what had happened, that I'd been bleeding internally, and at the same instant, I felt dizzy, like I'd pass out any instant.

Death, so near so many times before, was right there at the door, and I knew it. My legs buckled, but I refused to let the curtain of darkness draw across my mind. I crawled to the telephone to call an ambulance, then somewhere in the hazy reaches of consciousness, I realized the police would get in the act because I'd been stabbed, and I was sure, too, they'd see the holes in my arms from shooting drugs.

But there was only one thing to do. I dialed the ambulance service listed on the telephone book cover.

"Hello," I said weakly. "This is Gary Fisher." I gave them the address. "I'm having an appendicitis attack," I said. "Please come and take me to a hospital!"

Within minutes, the ambulance crew — and the police — were at my door.

Chapter Twelve

The medicos and the police knew at a glance what my problem was, but at that point, I didn't care if they saw the hole in my side or not. Ignoring me, an ambulance attendant tossed a question at one of the police officers.

"Suicide attempt?"

"Probably," came the answer, and moments later, they were loading me into that long, especially-equipped vehicle.

Let them think what they wanted. All I knew was that I needed help. But I wasn't prepared for what came next. I stared at the green walls of the emergency ward at King County Hospital in Seattle and wondered what could possibly happen now. Then the doctor came in, took a quick look at me, and shook his head.

"How long ago did this happen?" he asked me.

I tried to figure it out. "About eleven o'clock last night," I said. "Twelve-fourteen hours."

Again the doctor shook his head despairingly. "Why didn't you get in here sooner?"

I looked around. There weren't any cops in sight. "I was so loaded I didn't feel much," I explained. "I didn't think I was hurt so bad."

"We're going to have to operate on you," the doctor went on, "and I want you to realize this isn't going to be any picnic. There's no way to know what we'll find. It looks pretty bad."

"You're telling me I might not pull through?" I asked, figuring we might as well get it out in the open.

117

"That's right," he said. "But you sure won't make it without immediate surgery — I don't see how you could last more than an hour or so longer."

"Let's go!" I said, turning aside to vomit blackish bile.

The doctor asked me to sign a paper authorizing the surgery, and with shaky fingers I scratched my name on the sheet. Then, before they could wheel me into the operating room in another part of the hospital, the police had to have a few questions, too. I don't recall just what they wanted, except they were trying to pin the thing down — whether I was, indeed, an attempted suicide case, or if I'd been knifed. But the doctor didn't let it go on long.

"Gentlemen, this man is dying!" he broke in while they were quizzing me. "Every moment is vital! You'll have to save your questions till later." He didn't add anything about maybe there wouldn't be any 'later' for me, and I was glad he didn't. I was scared enough as it was; by the time they turned the ether on, I was convinced I'd never come out of it.

The surgeons cut me open from my chest to my navel, and what they found, I'm not sure. I was told the scissors had penetrated my stomach, bowel, and a kidney, but just barely missed my spleen. And I was also told something else.

"Your stomach has holes in it from all the drugs you've taken," the doctor who'd first examined me said. "You don't have much time to live, if you keep treating your body that way." The abuse which had become a way of life had finally caught up with me, and at that moment, I figured it was time to quit.

But before that, when I came out from under the anesthetic, the first face I saw was Larry Hillis, director of Teen Challenge. "Welcome back to the world, Gary," he said. "You know we've been praying for you."

I nodded, not trusting my tongue. I couldn't figure this out. Here I was, a Teen Challenge runaway, in trouble because I hadn't followed their precepts, yet they'd been praying for me. Incredible!

"We'll be looking for you back at the Center when you're well, Gary," Larry said then. "You know Jesus still loves you!"

Again I nodded, and raised my hand to thank him for caring. I was glad when he was gone; I felt unaccountably guilty for having let the Teen Challenge people down.

My most frequent callers were the cops. Although they hadn't mentioned my drug problems, the surgeons apparently told them there was no way I could have sunk those scissors that far into myself, and the police wanted me to squeal on the guy who did it, so they could pin attempted murder on him. But I wouldn't tell; I'd decided I wanted to get him myself, for putting me through all this misery, though I never saw him again.

After a term in the hospital, I was transferred to a recovery unit, or convalescent sanitarium, and there were no more cops swarming in and out to bug me about the stabbing. There were no more tubes down my nose and throat to keep me going. But there was some infection where they took the stitches out of the incision down my middle, leaving me with something like an open wound to be treated with medication from time to time.

I hadn't been there but a couple of days when I decided I needed some Seven-Up, and I asked one of the attendants to get me some. He knew from the medical record that I was a drug addict, so he got smart about it.

"You'd probably get hooked on it," he sneered, ignoring the request.

That made me mad. So I sneaked out the window of the hospital and went down the fire escape. I was wearing striped pajamas at the time — red, white and blue. I went straight to a bar, but the bartender had a rather hazy outlook on people visiting there in their P-J's, so I heeded his advice to "Get the hell out of here!"

Then I went to the drugstore down the street, walked through the front door, and direct to the pharmacy. I stood there looking like the American flag in full blaze, as the pharmacist walked up.

Without blinking an eye, he looked me over and said, "Can I help you?"

"Yes," I said, "I want a bottle of terpin hydrate codeine cough syrup."

He didn't even raise an eyebrow. He just turned to his stock, picked out a bottle, and pushed the register out for me to sign. What a great guy! So I took the medicine and went flaming out of the store, across the street to the supermarket to buy a bottle of beer, and took my place in line at the cash register.

There I stood in my striped pajamas, with several little old ladies ahead of me, and they looked at me like they were going to salute and sing the National Anthem any second.

Then I felt a heavy hand on my shoulder, spinning me around. "Where did you come from?" the voice — unmistakably the voice of authority — slapped at me.

I tried to sound casual. "From the hospital," I shrugged, as though it were an everyday occurrence.

"Well, you better get on back there," the store manager with the big voice said, and he grabbed my arm to haul me in that direction, without even paying for the beer. Outside, he just headed me towards the sanitarium, and let me go. So I went around to the back of the store, sat down between two garbage bins, and drank the cough medicine and the beer. I was high once again.

When I finally felt like it, some time later, I got up and headed back for my temporary home at the convalescent hospital, but when I climbed up to the window and poked my head in, there was Mister Attendant waiting for me. And that ended that. I was discharged right then and there, but not before I'd swiped a bottle of hydrogen peroxide and some bandages from my room to use in treating the open incision on my stomach.

For a while, the heavy words laid on me by the doctor at the county hospital kept me on the straight and narrow — far more so than anything else I'd encountered up to that time. There was also the disturbing routine of pouring peroxide into the lesion on my stomach, a daily practice until it finally cleared up. So I joined my friend, Bill, and sponged off him as I'd done before I went to Teen Challenge.

I thought of returning to Teen Challenge, but with the knowledge that Larry Hillis and the others knew I'd been playing games with them, I just couldn't face them.

Then I had an inspiration! I'd heard from Larry and others at the Center that Teen Challenge was also active in Los Angeles, an area I knew well. The thing to do was go to LA, where I would check in at Teen Challenge and get a new start, away from the morphine and heroin scene that had turned my world upside down, instead of just sideways.

And once more, I took advantage of Bill's generosity. I couldn't face traveling that distance on my thumb, as I'd done previously, and the prospect of a long bus trip wasn't appealing, either. So Bill sprung for a used car, and I traveled down the coast in the spring of 1966 in a style I'd never enjoyed before. By the time I got to southern California, however, the old urges were gnawing at my insides, so when I couldn't locate the right turn-off to report in at the Los Angeles Teen Challenge, I did find a turn-off that led me straight to a liquor store, and a big bottle of wine. I was sure this wouldn't hurt me at all — it wasn't like the pills and the needle. It would settle things down for me, and I could then find my destination.

What I didn't count on was letting the alcohol get the better of me, which took only a short time. How long I drove back and forth on the freeway, I don't know for certain, but it seems as if it went on for several days. Finally, the inevitable happened: I was picked up by the cops and arrested for drunk driving. But I had presence of mind enough to look up and call the Teen Challenge in Los Angeles. The response was terrific; they'd be right down!

The events that followed should have been enough to convince me, once and for all, of the value of the Teen Challenge philosophy. Two young men, one whose first name — like mine — was Gary, and the other, a Black called Roy, came to my cell and reached through the bars, held my hands, and prayed for me.

"You know that God forgives our sins," Roy told me, after their prayers.

I nodded. He'd have an awful lot to forgive in my case, but I didn't bother to point that out.

"Don't worry about a thing," Gary added. "We'll be on hand when you go to trial. And we'll have Jesus on our side!"

My case came up before the judge the next day, and by that time I was dried out from the binge I'd launched. I was also hurting from the after-effects, because the alcohol had awakened all the old cravings for drugs, and I could hardly wait to escape from custody.

True to their word, Gary and Roy were beside me when I faced the judge, and they were quietly urgent in their request to have me released to the guardianship of the Teen Challenge organization.

"I've traveled the same road," Gary told the judge. "I lived on pills, booze, heroin until the Lord Jesus Christ opened my mind one day and brought me to Teen Challenge. I've been a new man ever since, for I was born again." He placed his hand on my shoulder as we stood there facing the judge. "The same thing can happen to Gary Fisher, your Honor. It's a house of miracles."

Then it was Roy's turn, and the judge just sat there on his bench with his mouth open while Roy talked. "I was in it deep, your Honor," Roy said. "I was tried for murder, under the influence of drugs. My life was all mixed up, until I turned on to Jesus through Teen Challenge. Since that time," Roy paused and looked at me, his face radiant, "I've been set free, in more ways than one. I've dedicated my life to Jesus Christ, and your Honor, Gary Fisher was looking for Teen Challenge when he took a wrong turn. We'll see that God gives him the chance he deserves."

The judge was obviously impressed. "Gary Fisher," he said slowly, "I'm going to release you to the custody of these men, who represent this organization called Teen Challenge. See to it that I don't see your name on my register of cases again!"

"Yes, sir!" I smiled and shook hands with Gary and Roy, then turned and walked out with them. I was free once more.

But was I? Teen Challenge in Los Angeles turned out to be even more stringent than the one in Seattle. Yet, there was an unmistakable air of accomplishment behind the doors I walked through with Gary and Roy at my side. I saw, to my surprise, the happiest faces I'd ever glimpsed in my entire life. They were of all kinds — Spanish, Chinese, Negro, Anglo . . . just about every race you could think of, all mixed up in this one house together.

And talk about ambition! These guys were really getting it

on. They were studying the Bible together every day, planning to become ministers for the Lord, and some even working toward careers as missionaries, ready to go out and help the poor, and to help young kids get off the street. It didn't take any time at all to learn that many of them had been further along the road of evil than even I had been . . . they'd robbed and stolen and had beaten people over the head with clubs; they'd been guilty of purse-snatching and burglaries; they'd pulled armed robberies. Many of them had done time in prison.

Yet, after all that, here they were, wanting to do something right, and praising the Lord with unbelievable happiness etched in their smiling faces. I couldn't help wondering where it all came from, for though I'd played along in Seattle, even witnessed for Christ the way they wanted me to, I'd never really bought their program. I was jiving them. Could I play the same game here, as well?

Gary and Roy led me to the office, where I faced the stern but friendly face of Sonny Arguinzoni. "You've been given a second chance, Gary," he said. "I understand you've been on drugs, booze, the whole bit. Do you really want to make it — to get rid of those worthless habits?"

"I sure do!" I assured him. "That's why I called Teen Challenge."

His eyes searched me carefully. Then, as if on signal, Gary and Roy began a systematic ransacking of my clothing and the contents of my suitcase. "There just isn't room here at Teen Challenge for any of the stuff you've been using," Gary explained. "And that includes cigarettes." He wadded up the remains of a pack he'd found in my suitcase.

"Come on," Roy said then. "We'll find you a bed."

From that moment on, there simply wasn't a minute to worry about the drugs or the smokes or the booze I wasn't getting. The schedule was heavy, morning to night. But the guys around me were so genuinely happy and so intent on doing everything they could for others — including me — that life became a paradox . . . easy, and at the same time, rough.

There was a full schedule of work and activity during the days, and Bible school at night. There simply wasn't time to think about the old life. I got into Andraé Crouch's Addicts' Choir, and we traveled from churches to schools sharing our testimony of the saving grace of Jesus Christ.

I suppose you might say I was the clown of the group, without really meaning to be. In the first place, with my two front teeth missing, I was a sight to behold. Second, my testimony was so crazy, covering some of the things I'd gone through in my life, the kids would really turn on and laugh at and with me. And at the end of our program, they'd give us standing ovations and then stand in line and want to know more about the love of God.

We spent more time in church than we did sleeping. We were always out witnessing — many times on the streets, when there wasn't a church service scheduled. It was a good time in my life, and it went on for almost six months. I was really getting into the Bible study program, handicapped though I was when it came to reading. But I'd go up on top of the roof of our building in the afternoons and study, and I got such a good tan with this routine that the others thought I had to be sneaking off to the beach.

* * * *

There was plenty of good companionship among all of us at the Los Angeles Teen Challenge Center, including several real pals who would help me with big words and other things I didn't understand. Among those I came to know and like was a tall Spanish girl named Margret. I was disappointed, one day, to learn she'd left the Center; she'd just disappeared. I knew others were likewise disappointed, for all of us knew how close we were to the other side of life, how near we were to going back to the problems we'd had before.

A couple of nights later, Margret showed up at a service where we were singing and testifying, and when she slipped into the pew beside me I was pleased that she'd returned. Then she quietly showed me what she had in her hand — a big roll of twenty-dollar bills.

"Gary," she whispered, peeling off one of the twenties and slapping in into my hand. "I'll meet you after the service. Come on and live at my house, and we'll have a ball!'' And she slipped me a piece of paper with her address and telephone number.

The devotions went on, but my mind was elsewhere. I forgot all about what I was there for, and all I could think about was Margret's invitation to live it up. So when the service was over, I conned the guys into taking me to Margret's house.

"I just want to talk to her for a minute," I told them. "I think I can get her to come back to the Center."

Margret opened her door and let me in, and I looked at her and locked it behind me. She had a good-sized glass of whiskey waiting for me, and I tasted alcohol again for the first time in many months. Not long after, the fellows from Teen Challenge knocked on the door.

I refused to open it. "Go away!" I told them.

"We got to go, Gary," one of them told me through the locked door. "Come on, man. Let's get back to the Center!"

"No way!" I said. "You go ahead. I don't want to go back just now. Everything's cool here!"

"Please, Gary! You don't want to throw everything away. Come on with us!"

But I wasn't having any of that. "I'll be along later," I said. "Get lost!" I could hear them reluctantly going back to the car.

It was I, of course, who was lost. Margret didn't have any drugs, but there was plenty of whiskey, vodka, and beer, and I loaded up on it day after day. The first three or four days, I'd walk with Margret to the nearby liquor store, and everything was fine. But after seven or eight days of staying tanked up, I began to get physically sick. I could only stagger from one tree to the next, needing their support to keep me on my feet.

It went from bad to worse; toward the end of the second week, I could barely stand, and the business of getting to the liquor store was more crawling than walking. I'd been consuming a fifth of vodka every day, as well as occasional shots of whiskey and now and then a can of beer. It was simply more than my body could stand.

Margret, meantime, decided she'd had enough of me, and leaving me some of her cash, she simply disappeared. At the end of the second week I staggered into a bar near the store and ordered a double shot of bourbon, figuring I needed a stimulant to get me back on my feet. But it didn't work. I had less strength than ever, and what little energy I had left, I used to drag myself back to the house. I obviously had to have help, but Teen Challenge was now out of the question. Out of the past came the realization there was one group that would assist me without asking any questions.

I asked the operator for the AA number, and somehow, I managed to dial it. Within half an hour, two members of Alcoholics Anonymous came to the house and sat in the front room with me.

"If you'll get rid of that beer, we'll help you," one of them said. Then he laughed. "And I don't mean drink it!"

"Fine with me," I muttered. "Pour it down the drain!"

The second man did just that. "Is this your place, or someone else's?" he asked while the brew went gurgling down the sink.

I had to think a minute to come up with the answer, for my muddled brain didn't want to function. "Someone else," I mumbled. I was so weak I could hardly sit up, let alone talk.

"How about coming with us to the AA house?" the first man asked then.

"Sure!" I said thickly. "Let's go."

But I was already gone. The overdose of alcohol laid me out, and the two men had to carry me to their car. It must have taken me close to three days to sleep it off, with the help and attention of the AA members. Another three days, and I was cold sober. I was also ashamed of what I'd done. My six months of rehabilitation at Teen Challenge were down the tube. I began to wonder if I would ever straighten out my life, and I hated myself for being such a weakling. But I knew only one thing to do.

I thanked the AA people for their help, sneaked into the garage at the Teen Challenge Center, and got my car. Then I used the little money I had left from the binge with Margret, and bought some more booze. It was almost as if I had a compulsion to get myself picked up and put back in jail, because that's exactly what happened. And this time, the judge had no choice: six months in the county jail!

After a brief time, I was assigned to the Norwalk sub-station and began working in the garage there, servicing the county sheriff's automobiles. It sounds like a normal, routine job, but some of us assigned there added special effects.

Those cars got a thorough going over when we were working on them; we'd always pull out the back seat to look for marijuana or pills that people would stash when they were on the way to the slammer. And when we'd find a big old joint — what we called a ''bomber'' — we'd smoke it to get at least a good start on a high.

What's more we'd find pills, and I'd slap them under my tongue until I could hide them in the fly of my trousers, so I could save them up and get loaded later on.

One of the guys assigned there was a black named Dan, and he and I became close friends. One day we were looking for something we could get stoned on, and he found a couple of cans of 190-proof alcohol. There was a red skull and crossbones on it, and I knew what that meant.

''Man, this ought to bring on a real trip,'' Dan suggested.

''No way!'' I said. ''I ain't gonna drink that stuff — it's poison! Look at the label!''

''Oh, come on, man!''

''No, sir! I don't mind getting loaded, but I'm not looking for six feet under — not yet!''

''Tell you what,'' Dan said then. ''All you got to do is light a match to it and that'll burn the poison out of it. Go get us some orange pop to pour in it, and we can get stoned out of our minds — solid, man!''

''Well, okay,'' I finally agreed.

So Dan lit a match to the alcohol and let it burn for a little while, and I headed for the pop machine inside the nearby station headquarters. When I got back, we poured the pop into the hooch, and I looked at Dan, and he looked at me.

''Man,'' I said, ''you drink it first, and if you live, then I'll drink some, too.''

So Dan downed a big slug of the stuff, and he got ripped in no time at all — stoned out of his mind. I figured if that was all it did for him, that was what it would do for me. So I drank a big glass full of the mixture, and right away, I knew Dan must have a cast-iron stomach. I got so crocked I could hardly walk, and when Dan and I finally got back to our cell, I stretched out on my pallet and felt the whole bunk lifting up off the ground. The stuff was eating me alive inside!

All night long, I had nightmares — horrible dreams like the time I had the D-T's with all the lizards coming at me. Morning was a year in coming, but when it finally arrived, I went straight to the sergeant and told him I needed to go see a doctor — that I was sick with the flu. So they took me to the hospital, and the next thing I knew, I was in another familiar spot — a padded cell! That stuff had set me so wild, the doctors decided I was a mental case, so I was back where I'd been before, and wondering what it was all about.

The county jail's mental facility was in some ways the worst I'd been in, because the guys in the ward where I was assigned were hopeless cases. Some were like animals, going on all fours, and leaping at those around them like a mad dog would. There were heroin addicts, with collapsed veins from long dosing and arms covered with scabrous abscesses. Again, I had to watch every step to avoid getting involved with the homosexuality that was part of the ward.

It took me six weeks to get out of the mental ward. From there I was assigned to the county jail kitchen for KP duties.

During the time I was in the county jail, I got my buddies to write, to Bill, my old friend in Seattle, so I could con him into sending me money from time to time. Once, I told him it was to settle a traffic ticket I had to pay before they'd let me out. That story was worth $25. I don't recall all the stories I cooked up, but by the time I got out, I'd saved over a hundred bucks, courtesy of Bill's soft heart.

It took me no time at all to get loaded out of my mind on booze. Why I did it, I'm not sure, but I ended up at Teen Challenge around midnight and gave them my money for safe-keeping, and they let me have a bed for the night. But the next morning, I decided it was time for me to split. I picked up the cash, intent for some reason on heading once more for Seattle.

Chapter Thirteen

It took part of my cash to bail my car out of the sheriff's impoundment station, but I managed to get back to Seattle in that spring of 1967 with no problems. Once there, I settled down to the old life of playing pool, dropping pills, drinking, dancing, carousing around, and worst of all, hitting the needle again. But through it all, somehow I just couldn't get any fulfillment out of doing the things I once thought were cool.

I would say to myself, "I don't want to do it!" but I'd turn right around and stick a needle in my arm or use the money I'd keep borrowing from my friend, Bill, to pick up some uppers or downers to get loaded. I can remember getting in the car and driving sixty, seventy, even eighty miles an hour to get to a drugstore or to make a connection for some hard drugs, and I'd cry and beat the steering wheel saying, "I don't want to go! God help me! I don't want to go!" But I'd go anyway.

There seemed to be a force inside me, driving me into the very thing I wanted to avoid. I kept going backwards . . . I was crippled, in both mind and body . . . I couldn't think straight, because my mind was destroyed. I knew I needed help, needed it badly. But I couldn't get it together enough to know where to turn, even though I'd been helped before. Deep down I was ashamed to turn again to the agencies that had helped me in the past, Alcoholics Anonymous and Teen Challenge.

I was so mixed up at this point that it didn't much matter to me what kind of drugs I took. Going back to my old habits, I'd go into a drugstore and stand there hoping the druggist wouldn't recognize me. I'd ask him for a bottle of terpin hydrate, and then I'd try to talk to him about something else, so he wouldn't have time to think about whether he'd seen me in there before. I'd sign one of my phony names — Gary Kearney, Donald Kearney, Donald Fisher — and then I'd walk out with the terpin hydrate, and go in a bar and order a beer. In the bar's bathroom I'd sit on the toilet and drink the terpin hydrate with some lemon to keep from vomiting.

Lots of times it would come right back up, and I'd have to hold it in my mouth and swallow it again; I was in pain, and I needed that drug inside me to stem the misery. I'd go to Bill's then, and lie down with the same fears, the same torments that I'd had when I started my daily routine. I'd wait for the next night to come, so I could drink more terpin hydrate or shoot some morphine, or perhaps some heroin or maybe get high on some kind of pills. I was nothing but a trash-can addict, willing to take anything to get loaded.

It was a miserable existence. Everyone who knew me had long since given up on me — my mother and stepfather, aunts and uncles, my brother. People who saw me coming down the street would cross over to the other side. I owed money to everyone I knew, and I saw these people more than I wanted — they were always after me to try to get it back. If it hadn't been for Bill, giving me cash from time to time, I don't know what I'd have done.

There was no way, of course, this could go on indefinitely. There came a night when I was out of cash, out of drugs, and had nowhere to turn. I laid there on my bed and cried for a long time, aware that my life was in ruins, and I was doing nothing about it besides helping it to happen. I got out my outfit, but I didn't have any drugs for a fix, so I sat there a while and squirted water out of the syringe at the cowboys cavorting on the television.

The pains were getting to me, as they always did when my body rebelled at not being drugged. Finally, at two in the morning, I reached for the telephone and in desperation, dialed the number for Alcoholics Anonymous. I don't know what I expected. Maybe just the fact I knew they'd send someone to me made me do it.

Between the time I called and the arrival of the AA member sent to help me, I looked all through the house for anything to drink, but there wasn't a drop to be had anywhere. So I emptied all of Bill's shaving lotion I could find into a glass and drank that, and I was feeling pretty bad when my visitor arrived.

He was Black and full of love and understanding, and he was fantastic. His name was Lon, and although he could see for himself what a genuine first-class failure I was, he refused to recognize that side of me.

"You have the potential for a great life, a wonderful life," Lon said to me after he'd made sure there wasn't any booze in the place to tempt me. "All you have to do, Gary, is believe you can make it.

"Let me give you the Serenity Prayer," Lon said. "It is one of the greatest helpers any man can use. Here — I'll read it to you." I saw that he held a small card in his hand, and I was glad he offered to read it to me — the only way I could get its message.

"God grant me," Lon read, then looked up to make sure I was listening; I was. "God grant me the serenity to accept the things I cannot change; the courage to change the things I can; and the wisdom to know the difference."

I nodded. I'd heard it before, but I'd long since forgotten it. "Thanks, Lon," I said. "I appreciate your help."

For four hours, Lon stayed with me, and by the end of that time, I'd told him many of the things that had happened to me. In fact, it was like giving my testimony at a street meeting, except now I had an audience of only one.

"Remember, you can change your life, Gary," he told me in parting. "Think it over. The best times in your entire adult life have been when you've worked with Teen Challenge. Don't you think it's time you gave that another try?"

He was right, and I knew it. I threw some things in my suitcase, just as I'd done so many times before, scratched the three words, "Will call you," on a note for Bill, and I went directly to the Teen Challenge Center, where Dave Torrez was now in charge. It was good to be back.

"Of course we'll help you, Gary," Dave told me. "But you

know you're going to have to do your part, too."

"I know, Dave," I told him. "I'll do my best." I meant it.

But it didn't take long for me to get right back in the same old rut. I'd go snipe hunting for roaches, just like before, so I could steal a smoke now and then. I'd swipe someone's bottle of after-shave lotion now and again, and sneak off somewhere and drink it. However, getting loaded didn't make it for me anymore. I started getting a lot more kick, a lot more satisfaction out of following the Teen Challenge schedule and being commended for my cooperation and efforts. I was finally getting it together, including testimony and witnessing at our street meetings and other functions. It was probably five or six weeks later that Dave posed a question.

"Gary, the Bar-Forty-one Ranch needs some guys to help them this summer — counselors and that sort of thing. Would you like to go out and give them a hand?"

I thought about it, recalling the days when I'd done ranch-type work at The Hacienda — work I'd really enjoyed. "Great," I said. "I'm your man!"

So I was assigned to the ranch — a set-up not unlike The Hacienda, where boys from juvenile hall were sent to give them some worthwhile experience and guidance. I was a counselor, and for a time, I did fine. I enjoyed the open air, and I liked working with the younger boys. I did start smoking again, but I didn't think that really mattered.

There were ten boys, ages twelve to fifteen, who were my particular responsibility. I had my own room, in the same building where they stayed, and I felt like I was finally amounting to something. We'd go out every day to do our work assignments, with the boys doing the work, and me supervising. Our little crew would clean out the cow manure from the barn, and we'd go out into the mountains and clean up the fallen limbs and brush and the debris that unthinking people left behind them. It was a good life.

But these were boys who, like me, were never content to stay on proper pathways. One Saturday when we were out in the woods, I heard a scream, and I saw Owen — a real good boy — running across a clearing, and about thirty yards behind him was another boy, Rick, with a good sized tree limb in his hand. Rick was chasing Owen, trying to hit him over the head with his club.

I took off running and managed to get between them before Rick could do any damage, and I turned him around and hit him in the face, knocking him down. Then I took the club away, and marched them back where they'd been.

"All right, where is it?" I asked. I knew what to look for. I could smell it on them, and I could see it on Rick's face. I'd been there myself.

Sheepishly, the boys showed me their plastic bags, and the glue they'd been sniffing. So I wrapped it all up and stuck it into my cowboy boots, making sure Rick wasn't going to do Owen in again. I'd sobered him somewhat when I knocked him down, and he admitted he'd thought Owen was some sort of monster trying to get his glue away from him.

"Get on back to the house!" I told them both. "I'll deal with you later."

From that moment, a strange thing happened. That glue started talking to me. I could plainly hear a voice saying, "Gary, why don't you go ahead and try a little bit . . . sniff a little yourself tonight, when nobody's looking. You could do it right now. Go ahead, Gary."

The rest of my crew were off in the woods, and didn't need me, as they knew what was expected of them. So I opened up one of the plastic bags and took out the glue, and started sniffing — the routine I'd been introduced to at The Hacienda. Here I was — the counselor, the guy who was supposed to help these kids get straight, and I not only took the glue away from them, but started sniffing it myself. It was the old Gary Fisher all over again.

I'd found a spot between two big trees, and after I'd broken the glue tubes open and put them inside the plastic bag, it didn't take long for things to start happening.

First, I started hearing funny sounds, like a mini-siren on a police car. Then, all of a sudden something very small started to come from high in the sky, coming to me ever so slowly, but growing larger and larger until I could see it plainly. It turned out to be a man, standing twenty feet tall and five feet off the ground, wearing a purple robe with a white inner cloth. From pictures I'd seen at Teen Challenge and in people's houses, I knew this giant of a man. I knew the long hair, the neatly-trimmed beard. I knew that Jesus Christ was speaking to me.

There I was, on my knees in the grass between the trees, looking up with tearful eyes as my visitor started telling me about myself.

"You've taken the wrong road, Gary," the gentle voice said, "and you've done many bad things, but you can change all that. You can be of great help to young people, if you give your life to helping sinners. You can be a minister of God. You can, Gary — you can."

And then, in the space of an instant it seemed, this giant standing over me opened His mouth and He went through my whole life, laying it out before me in all its sordid reality. Gasping in amazement, I tried to speak, wanting to verify that I was, indeed, in the presence of the Son of God. But words wouldn't come.

As suddenly as He had appeared, He was gone. The whole episode had blown my mind. I longed to see Him again, and talk to Him about my life and what I could do with it. So I emptied some more glue into the bag and sniffed and sniffed, but He wouldn't come back. Instead, I went into a completely different kind of trip, far more frightening than the first.

I was sitting there with my back against a tree, and all around me, the leaves started coming off the trees and began dancing around on the ground in a circle. Now, I was the giant, in my own little kingdom, but when the leaves began talking to me, their message was chilling.

"You're going to blow it all, Gary Fisher, if you don't stop sniffing glue and taking all those other drugs. You're going to blow it!" I wanted to answer them, but as before, the words wouldn't come. I could only sit there and watch, as one by one, the leaves settled down and no longer danced in front of me. The high was wearing off.

Let me emphasize, here and now, that glue-sniffing is no way to go — the chances of anyone else having a vision such as I had on that trip are totally nil . . . just as I was unable to produce the image of Jesus Christ the second time around, I'm sure no one else could ever duplicate my experience. If you want to see the Lord, sniffing glue is the *very last* thing you should do. In my case, when the effects of the glue had worn off, I took my crew back to the ranch house, still frightened by my afternoon adventure.

And the very next day, when everyone got up and went to church, I said I was sick, that I didn't want to go. I was sick, all right; but it was a different kind of sickness. As soon as everyone was gone, I found a bottle of after-shave lotion in the bathroom, drank it, and started getting high. Then I went searching through the rooms, gathering up all the after-shave and under-arm deodorant and anything else I could find that would get me loaded. I collected probably twenty-five dollars worth of the stuff, and then I poured it all into a pitcher, cut the deodorant cans in half and poured them into the pitcher, too; then I sat there and watched the concoction bubble.

Deep inside, I realized that drinking the stuff would probably kill me. But I didn't care; I had that familiar compulsion to get stoned, to forget once again who I was and what I was and why I was where I was. I drank it all.

It almost took the top of my head off, to start, and I could feel it chewing my stomach up when it hit — just eating me alive. I was loaded, but good! And before the boys and the other counselors returned from church, I was green and vomiting again and again, and was still at it when everyone came back. I hadn't bothered to put away the evidence of my misdeeds, and within minutes the supervisors had me in the office to give me my walking papers. I felt terrible, not so much about being fired, but seeing the disappointment — even anger — in the faces of the boys I'd worked with. They had looked up to me.

Deeply depressed, I hitchhiked to Seattle. I was sure there was only one way I could overcome the burdens that buried me so deep in despondency — I would go back to Teen Challenge. The rigid discipline there, and the exposure to the teachings of Jesus Christ, would surely straighten my path.

"I'm sorry, Gary," Dave Torrez told me quietly. "I just don't feel you're ready for Teen Challenge yet. You have a record of backsliding that won't quit. Maybe someday . . . but not now. I'm sorry!''

Bitterly, I turned to go. I hadn't expected this — being turned down by Teen Challenge. I'd made my bed; now I had to lie in it. I stumbled out the door, not knowing where I could go, or what I could do. I had some cash; the wages at the ranch weren't big, but I'd been paid off when I was fired. And I knew where I could sponge some more cash to go with it. So I took a cab to Bill's place, using the key I always carried to let myself in. I waited till Bill came home, conned him out of a twenty-dollar bill, and then called Jack — my old buddy who'd turned me on to morphine.

He came by and picked me up and we bought sixty dollars worth of the stuff that night, then went to a shooting gallery, where everybody was fixing. We all sat around a big round table with our dope laid out in front of us. We'd put it in our spoons and cook it and shoot a vein. But every time there was a knock on the door, everyone would jump up and head for the windows, ready to split. Like the others, I became paranoid, so I took off.

A few days before, I'd had a good job working with kids on a ranch . . . good food, good atmosphere, good opportunity to influence others in the right direction. Now, I was back to the degradation of a skid row addict. I had nowhere to turn. Teen Challenge didn't want me. Alcoholics Anonymous had been helpful, but I knew they could offer me no more than a temporary helping hand. If I'd been sincere in my acceptance of Jesus Christ as Lord and Master, I could have turned to Him . . . but I wasn't. I'd just gone through the motions, and for that reason, I was ashamed to call on Him now.

So I wandered down a lonely Seattle street. It was raining, the dismal numbing rain that could only add to my burden of distress. As I walked, I heard gospel music, a sound that took me back to the times I'd sung with the Addicts' Choir in Los Angeles. I found that it came from the basement of a church nearby, and as though someone was guiding my steps, I went down the stairs and slipped in the door.

I couldn't believe it! There, his black face shining with

feeling, was my old friend, Andraé Crouch — the Addicts' Choir director — leading the singing in his always fervent way. I had barely slipped inside the door, when he deserted his post at the front of the room, and strode briskly toward me, while the gospel music continued to fill the air.

"Gary!" he said. "Welcome! It's good to see you!"

I nodded, not trusting my tongue to come up with the right words.

"Gary, you know that Jesus still loves you!" Andraé said then. "I know you have problems, and I want you to know that I really have a burden on my heart to help you. We're all going to pray for you, Gary!"

I couldn't stand it. His words hit me like nothing ever had before. Without a sound, I turned and ran up the stairs. Behind me, I could hear Andraé shouting at me. "We'll pray for you, Gary! Call me when you really want help!" It was just like something was chasing me.

Somehow, I got to Bill's place, but I was so frightened I didn't know what was happening. I crawled under the bed, my heart pounding against the springs over me. I was sure the cops were surrounding the place, and I was sure they'd find me. So I crept out and got into the closet to hide there. When you're paranoid, everything gets really weird. I wanted to hide, yet I knew I couldn't. I knew what was the matter, and yet I refused to face my problem. You can't hide from God.

Chapter Fourteen

As always, the only thing I could think of to do was to run. Whenever I got into trouble, my first thought was if I went back to where I'd been before, I'd leave the trouble behind. It had never worked, but I refused to face that fact.

But that fall, 1967, I told my friend, Bill, once again that I was going back to LA. If Teen Challenge in Seattle wasn't having any part of me, perhaps the same organization in Los Angeles would feel differently. I had done better as a person during my months at the LA Teen Challenge than at any other time in my life. I had completely forgotten how badly I had bombed out of their program the last time I was there, conning them to take me to Margret's and then going on a two-week bender that wound up with me spending six months in jail.

So I said goodbye to Bill and got on a California-bound bus, my pockets full of terpin hydrate. It seemed like an endless trip, although it was by far the fastest time I'd ever made between Seattle and Los Angeles. The bus pulled into the station at three in the morning, but by then, I'd already made my plans. I had Andraé Crouch's home telephone from my days in his Addicts' Choir, so without hesitating, I dialed the number.

A sleepy voice answered. "Hello."

"Andraé," I said, "this is Gary Fisher. You said to call when I needed help."

"Praise God!" Andraé exclaimed. "Where are you, Gary?"

"At the Greyhound bus station, downtown," I told him. "I —"

"I'll be right down. Just sit tight!"

I waited, lighting one cigarette after another. My nerves were raw. I'd used up all my terpin hydrate by early evening of the preceding day, so I'd been without drugs for close to eight hours, and I was hurting. But almost before I knew it, a smiling Andraé Crouch was extending a friendly hand to me.

"You've just proved something again, Gary! I knew it, I've always known it, but it needs reinforcing once in a while."

I wondered how this man could be so full of exuberance at such an ungodly hour of the morning. "What's that?" I asked, not really caring.

"The power of prayer! I've been praying for you ever since I saw you in Seattle. Now, here you are — the answer to my prayers!" And with a companionable hand on my shoulder, "Come on, let's go home."

We got into his little green VW, and as we started driving toward the freeway, he turned toward me and shook his head. "Gary, you look like you're sixty years old. We've just got to do something about you!"

If I looked sixty, I felt ninety. "Andraé," I said. "I don't care what happens — I am going to make it!"

"Praise God!" And then Andraé did a strange thing, unless you knew him well, as I did. He reached over into my shirt pocket and pulled out the pack of cigarettes nestling there. With one quick toss, he launched them out the window. "Hate to be a litterbug, Gary, but it's for a good cause!" he said, smiling. He held out his hand again for me to grasp. "Welcome home!"

I was so exhausted physically that I went to sleep immediately when we reached the Crouch home, despite the pains that were dogging me. And next morning, he took me to the familiar site where I'd enjoyed some of the most productive months of my life . . . the Los Angeles Teen Challenge Center.

It had changed but little, and while I was not exactly welcomed with open arms, I was given the opportunity — thanks in part to Andraé— to stay.

I was grateful myself for the heavy grind imposed on us, for it allowed no time for thinking about the problems all of us were trying to overcome. The Teen Challenge doctrine that idle time is an addict's poison was being put to good use, and the rougher the routine, the easier it was for me to hang in there. I'd failed so miserably . . . so many times . . . that I was sincerely determined to make it this time.

As for Andraé, bless him, he was using reverse psychology on me that I was unaware of at the time. "Gary, you're never going to make it!" he'd tell me. "You're nothing but a fly-by-night!"

That made me mad. The more he told me I was hopeless, the more determined I was to make it. "I *am* going to make it!" I told him, "even if it's just to prove it to you!"

The weeks slid by, and I couldn't help feeling some pride in myself. Although I was conscious that I had not yet accepted the fullness of Christ's spirit into my heart, at least I really was cooperating with the Teen Challenge program. I was proving to Andraé Crouch that this time Gary Fisher *was* going to make it.

And I was even more proud when Don Hall, the TC Director, called me into his office one day. I was uptight at first, for I couldn't recall having done anything out of line that would be cause for discipline. I wondered what I was being called in for.

But Don put me at ease immediately. "Gary," he grinned at me, "did you know you're one of the ugliest specimens we have around this place?"

"Sure!" I grinned back. "Do I get a trophy or something?"

"No," Don said. "You get a couple of new teeth. We're all tired of looking at that colossal gap in your mug. Okay if I set up a dental appointment for you?"

"You — you're going to —" I gasped. "That — that's great!" I was really excited. I'd no longer have to stand in embarrassment before the kids at the schools where we'd go to testify. I would no longer look like a madman. I could hold my head up with the others.

The two new teeth made me more determined than ever to make it, and for the next several months, Teen Challenge was my entire life. I could face others with confidence; I could look back on my years of hopelessness and shake my head in wonder that I'd actually survived. Finally, the time came when we decided to expand the ministry we had created. So six of us from the Los Angeles Teen Challenge went to San Diego, setting up our own worship center in, of all places, a former bar, in a location where we could attract a lot of the very people we had set out to enlist in the service of the Lord.

It was at the modified bar in San Diego that I met Max Rappaport, director of Teen Challenge in Garden Grove — an Orange County suburb of Los Angeles. I felt I was really getting my life together now, so when Max asked me to join the unit there, I was happy to accept. Teen Challenge in Garden Grove was different from any such place I'd been in before. It was more open, more for the guy who had already made it. I felt it was a compliment, an honor to be asked to participate in that group.

* * * *

I worked with Teen Challenge in Garden Grove as the evangelistic director for about four months, and this was one of the best of times for me. We were really getting it on, and three of us decided it was time to expand our ministry. We'd heard that California's Big Sur area was a haven for addicts, so this seemed the best goal to set for ourselves. We took off early one summer morning in 1968 — Tommy Madison, who owned the pickup we were driving; Ralph Coker, who'd been at the center for several months; and I — the leader, since I was evangelistic director of the center. Max gave me twenty dollars to meet our physical needs, and Ralph had sixty dollars of his own, so we were all set to share the message of evangelism.

We had a fine time as we drove up the coast, enjoying the beautiful scenery, talking and cracking jokes as we rode along. But it was a long drive, and by the time we'd reached our destination, the subject of how hot it was came up, and someone joked about how good a cold beer would taste. I voiced my first reaction quickly.

"No way, man!"

But then I started thinking about it, and the other guys were obviously thinking about it, too. So we hashed it over for ten minutes or so.

"After all, it's only one. Can't hurt anything."

We drove down to the bottom of the hill we were on, went on

into Monterey, and I went into a store to buy one beer for each of us. But once inside, the old urges started prodding me. After all, I told myself, they come in six-packs. I'll just buy a six-pack for us — it's a better deal.

Well, the store didn't have the regular cans in six-packs — all they had were the big half-quart cans, so I picked up a six-pack of those, looking around guiltily to see if anyone was watching me. Then I ran and jumped into the pickup. I'd like to let Ralph Coker tell the story at this point, as he set it down in a recent letter:

"Here we were, 350 miles from Garden Grove, with a six-pack of beer and paranoid. We drove and drove, trying to find a spot to drink it; finally coming upon a grove of trees, we walked out into the middle, and crouched down and drank our beer.

"Well, enough is enough, we told ourselves, and decided to make our way back to Big Sur. But Gary wanted to stop at the next liquor store. The transformation from a modern day Dr. Jekyll to Mr. Hyde was beginning to take place.

"Gary had been Tommy's idol for a long time at Teen Challenge, placing him on a spiritual pedestal, so he objected to Gary's idea of going back to the liquor store. Nevertheless, Gary prevailed, claiming, 'This day is already shot since we have booze on our breath. Tomorrow will be another day and we will get down to witnessing then.' "

Ralph Coker's report of the event continues: "Gary's idea of another drink or two was a fifth of vodka and then another and another. For Gary, there was no stopping. His personality became demanding and coarse. It seemed as if his mind would fade in and out, sometimes knowing you and other times not.

"But the most drastic of all changes was his overwhelming desire to kill himself. All reasoning was futile as Gary time after time attempted to jump out of the car as we sped along at sixty-five miles per hour."

I don't recall wanting to do away with myself, but I'm sure Ralph is correct in his recollection. What I do recall is the knowledge that the devil was sitting on my shoulder, just like when I was a little kid. We forgot about our mission, and instead of returning to Big Sur, we drove on up to San Francisco, with me almost totally blacked out from the alcohol I'd consumed. Let's have Ralph pick up the report again:

"We watched Gary deliberately pick a fight with a truck driver in a truck stop cafe. Another time, we had stopped at a gas station, and finding the men's rest room door locked, Gary proceeded to use the door for relief. The woman gas station attendant promptly turned a water hose on him full force, leaving Gary soaking from head to toe.

"Pity would barely describe my feelings for Gary at that moment. Soaking wet, red-eyed, and with a mind only half-functioning, I saw a man totally different and changed from four days ago.

"As I look back now, it seems as if Gary was driven by the unseen forces of hell. A demonic oppression that robbed him of his capacity to reason was ever-present with him. He seemed to be controlled as a puppet by Satan himself. And his desire to end his life could only have been motivated by demonic powers."

Ralph Coker is today the much-respected Director of Extended Outreach for Orange County Teen Challenge of Southern California. I can only look backward and confirm his report.

God's hand was surely on us, for we did return to Southern California's Orange County, and without wrecking ourselves beyond what we'd already done. Ralph went back to Teen Challenge, but there was no way I could do that. I simply could not bring myself to face Max Rappaport, after acting as I had. So I wandered in the streets for a time, uncertain where to turn, what to do with myself.

Not long after that, Ralph got involved with the Webster House in Anaheim, and when I heard about it I went there.

"Welcome, Gary!" He was such a fine person to be around, always treating me groovy. "Come on in!"

My clothes were in tatters, nothing but rags, and Ralph noticed this quickly. "Hey, man, try some of my clothes on," he offered. Ralph probably had a twenty-eight inch waist, and couldn't have weighed more than a hundred and forty pounds; his body frame was much smaller than mine. Yet, when I put on his clothes, they hung on me like a scarecrow's — that's how thin and messed up I was. But I thanked Ralph for the clothing he let me have, and I arranged with him to stay at the Webster House, a haven for misfits like me.

There was work to do as part of their program, so I began painting a house for a lady and started having all kinds of terrible stomach cramps. That meant a trip to the doctor, who gave me some relaxer pills. Being an old pillhead, I ignored the directions and downed a handful of them at once. This of course set me off again, and despite Ralph Coker's objections, I was kicked out of the Webster House.

Again, I wandered around, but by now I was familiar enough with the various organizations which were sincerely trying to do something for the down-and-outers, the drug addicts, the flotsam and jetsam of the streets. So I checked in at one of them called "Families in Christ," and they put me to work. Their arrangement was to find jobs for those involved in their program, but to take all the money earned to support their ministry.

I went to work in a laundry that cleaned sheets for hospitals, on the night shift. All night long I'd load sheets onto trucks — thirteen of them in the eight-hour stretch. Then I'd go back to the home and turn over the sixty-five dollars a week I was making. But like so many times before, I got all messed up again. I'd sneak off during the daytime when I should have been resting, and buy cough medicine — the kind without codeine, but with an alcohol base — and then beer, and I'd get drunk.

Then one day I ran into a guy I'd known in my earlier years in Lòs Angeles, and he turned me on to LSD. I'd never tripped on it before, but I was so busy running away from myself that anything was all right with me at this point.

Ted sat me in a chair before slipping me the acid. "This is going to be some kind of a trip for you," he said, standing there before me. "As you start entering into this trip, Gary, I want you to remember that I am God. I want you to watch me — I'm going to pull electricity out of the sky, and you're going to see all kinds of colors."

So I watched him, and just as he said, he started pulling all these colors out of the sky — electricity and fire and all kinds of weird psychedelic effects. Then my friend who claimed he was

God put me under a spell, and I thought I was going to go nuts. He scared me so bad I couldn't even talk for three days.

And at the end of that time, a friend from the Garden Grove Teen Challenge named Mike picked me up and was ready to take me to a mental institution — I was that far gone. But I pleaded with him, and because he wanted to help, he took me instead back to Teen Challenge in Los Angeles. I hoped maybe they hadn't heard about my latest escapades. But word travels fast.

"Look, Gary," Don Hall told me, "we just can't keep you here. You've blown it — I don't know how many times. You're nothing but a stoned reject, and there's no way our staff can put up with you." His face was grim. "You've had your chance, more chances than just about anybody I know. But now we've had it up to here! " And he drew his hand across his throat in emphasis.

I nodded, fighting back bitter tears. Again, I had no choice but to accept the verdict. He was right. There was no more hope for me. I turned unsteady feet toward the door, and once outside it I began running desperately down the street . . . toward nowhere.

Chapter Fifteen

"Gary! Wait up! *Gary!*"

I was running so hard I sensed rather than heard my name being called. Did I imagine it? I kept running.

"Gary! Slow down! Wait a minute!"

I heard it plainer this time. No mistake. Someone was chasing me. I did slow down, but more because I was getting winded than because I wanted to see who was calling me.

Then I heard the footsteps, and a gentle voice from the past. "Hey, man — what you runnin' for?"

I felt a firm hand on my shoulder, so I stopped, turned around, and looked into the face of George Smith, a young black man I remembered from when I'd been in the Los Angeles Teen Challenge the first time.

"It's no use, man," I said. "I guess I'll be running the rest of my life."

"Sure," he agreed, "running for Jesus!" George held out his hand to me then — not to be shaken, but to lead, as one would lead a confused child.

"Gary," George said, as he slowly drew me toward him there on the sidewalk, "you prayed for me last year, and you helped bring me to the Lord. I don't know what's troubling you now, but whatever it is, I want to help." The black hand squeezed mine reassuringly. "What can I do?"

"It's too late, George," I said miserably. "I've had my chance — more chances than anyone has a right to expect. I've blown them all. It's no use!"

"You're forgetting something important, Gary!"

I looked at my friend, recalling the way he'd come to Teen Challenge — a derelict like me without self-respect, without hope, ready to grasp at any straw he could find to keep from drowning in a sea of torment. How much different he looked now — calm, self-assured, almost stately in his personal dignity.

"I am?" I didn't much care.

"Yes!" he said quietly. "You're forgetting the source of all our strength."

I was feeling too sorry for myself to realize what he meant, though I certainly should have known. "Huh?"

" 'If we confess our sins, He is faithful and just to forgive us our sins, and to cleanse us from all unrighteousness.' " George nodded his head and smiled. "That's from First John, Chapter One, Verse Nine," he said. "Gary — come with me. Please!"

I hesitated. What was the use? I'd let everyone down. I'd let Jesus down, too. Would He really forgive?

"Gary, I want you to come back with me to the chapel and get on your knees and pray that the Lord Jesus Christ will help you. It's the only way!"

I realized suddenly that while he'd been talking and I'd been thinking, George had been slowly leading me back to the Teen Challenge building. We were almost there.

"They'll just ask me to leave," I protested weakly.

"Not if you're in the chapel, praying to the Lord to forgive your sins. Come on."

I let him lead me through the hall to the large room the Teen Challenge organization called its chapel. At the front of the room we both got on our knees, and before I could open my mouth, George made a simple appeal. ·

"Dear Lord," he said, "sometimes we ask some mighty big things of you, and we don't always do our part to make things happen. But right now, Lord, all we ask is that you listen. Listen, Lord — a lost sheep has come home to the fold."

He paused, and I knew it was my turn to pray, but I couldn't find any words. Instead, tears filled my eyes and started rolling down my cheeks. I knew I'd done wrong. I'd done wrong countless times. I wanted to ask God to forgive me for what I'd done, but the words wouldn't come.

Then I felt a hand on my shoulder, and thinking it was George urging me to get on with my prayer, I looked up through my tears and saw that another man had joined us there at the altar. I recognized him as Bill Minor, who — like George — had come to Teen Challenge when I'd been there before.

"Gary," Bill said, taking me by the hand as George had done, "do you really want to make it for the Lord?"

I nodded, not trusting my voice at first, and then I let it all out. "Yes!" I shouted. "I really do!"

"Look, Buddy," Bill said, "I'm going to take you down to the Anaheim Center." He pulled me to my feet. "I'm going to sic the Holy Ghost on you and let Him take care of you, and you're going to make it!"

The way Bill said them, those were the most encouraging words I'd heard in a long time. There was an unmistakable conviction in his voice. He meant it!

I'd heard that Bill was involved with the Teen Challenge Center in Anaheim, so I had a pretty good idea what I'd be getting into, but I was ready. If George Smith could get the Lord to listen long enough to send Bill Minor in to offer to take me there, the least I could do was try.

"I'll have to make some arrangements," Bill said then. "I'll send someone to pick you up tomorrow."

All the joy and excitement that had gripped me momentarily began to surge away. Why did everything have to be 'tomorrow'? And where would I go till then?

"You can stay here with me tonight, Gary," George said to me. "We'll pray together some more."

Bill nodded, extending his hand. "God bless you, Gary," he said. "See you tomorrow."

After the experiences of the past few days, including the temporary dread of being put in another mental institution following the LSD trip, I was exhausted, and sharing George's room was a blessing I hadn't counted on. There was an air of peace there; George had really gotten it on for the Lord. The time passed quickly, and before I knew it, I was bidding goodbye to my black brother who'd rescued me when everything was lost.

"Thank you, George," I said, holding his hand in both of mine.

"Don't thank me — thank Jesus!" he said, his dark eyes glowing.

I nodded. "Thank you, Jesus!" I said, and turned to go.

In the car, Larry Reed, who'd been sent to pick me up, was equally enthusiastic. "We're really glad to have you, Gary," he said. "Bill told me he knows you can make it, and we'll all help you, because we're all the same in the eyes of Jesus. We all love each other in the Lord!"

"I sure hope I can make it this time," I said.

"You can, Gary! You can!" Larry turned the car onto the freeway that would take us to Anaheim. We drove in silence for a while, and then came another pronouncement. "You might as well know it, Gary," he said seriously. "Bill has already received a couple of calls warning him to cut you loose." He suddenly grinned at me. "You sure have some reputation, old buddy!"

"I've been through a lot," I admitted, "But I really do want to get straightened out with the Lord." I shuddered, thinking of all I'd experienced. "I know if I don't make it this time, that's it. So with a little help. . ."

"Right!" Larry slapped my knee reassuringly. "Especially Jesus! He can make it happen." And then, as if remembering the warnings that were already coming in, "But you're right, actually. If you don't make it now, you never will. Just hang in there for Jesus, and it will come out okay."

But I couldn't help wondering — would it really work out for me, after all? Did I really have enough faith in the Lord to keep me on the straight path, after all the times I'd faltered?

Once we reached the Teen Challenge Center in Anaheim, things looked up. The fellows there welcomed me with open arms, showing a love I wouldn't have believed could exist, especially since they knew my track record.

"Welcome, Gary!"

"Praise the Lord, the prodigal son has come home!"

"Thank you, Jesus, for showing him the way!"

Those were just some of the words that surrounded me when

Larry and I arrived. The love that poured forth from those fellows was simply overwhelming. But I knew from experience I'd have to stand the test of time, and I could only hope that these sincere Christians would, indeed, be able to help me make the grade.

The outreach of love and action from the Orange County Teen Challenge, then located in Anaheim, now in the city of Orange, could be the subject of a number of books. Great things were — and still are — being done there, in laying new paths for the misguided and bringing them into a completely transformed way of life. I remembered Bill Minor's words: "I'm going to let the Holy Spirit take care of you!" It seemed to me the Holy Spirit had invaded that entire TC Center.

Our routine, although similar to that which I'd followed in the centers in Seattle and Los Angeles, seemed to have more life in it. We would get up in the morning and all pray together, and then we'd go out and do our ministry. We wouldn't wait for things to happen — we made them happen!

More than once I heard rumors that people who knew me and knew I'd come to Anaheim had called Bill with the same unhappy message: "Don't try to keep Gary Fisher there! He'll just blow it again. Get rid of him before he brings you all kinds of trouble."

But Bill, according to the reports that filtered down to me, had an answer ready for them. "No, I'm going to keep him," Bill would say. "I'm going to pray for him and God's going to use him. The past is buried, and Gary's going to make it this time!"

It gave me confidence to know that Bill had confidence in me . . . and in the power of Jesus Christ to work through me. And even if I hadn't yet found all the answers I wanted, I was ready to do anything I could for Bill, to justify his faith in me.

We had what we called a "school team" — a group, similar to the one at LA, set to go out and witness for Christ at various schools in the area. Bill assigned me to the school team, which I felt was an honor, and not long after, I began to lead the songs in our services. It was the most gratifying thing I'd done yet; there was just so much joy in serving the Lord in that group that everyone seemed to be caught up in it. And of course, as in the other Centers, there just wasn't time to go off in some wrong direction.

I shared a room with Randy Burks and we got along beautifully. He was a good influence on me; there's no question about the fact that I needed all the good influences I could get. I still hadn't been able to accept the idea I could turn my problems over to the Lord; I guess I thought they were too big for Him. But I was content to follow the program and walk the straight path laid out for us at the Teen Challenge Center.

* * * *

One day, in mid-1969, I went into Ralph Coker's room — Ralph, who had been with me on the trip to Monterey when I'd fallen by the wayside, was now a part of Anaheim TC — and I was sitting there, sniveling about all my problems, and how I wasn't ever going to be able to amount to anything because I'd been deprived of the proper education and the proper influences when I was growing up. I was really wallowing in self-pity, when he suddenly looked up and smacked me right between the eyes with some well-chosen words.

"You think you're the only one who has problems?" Ralph said to me. "Why don't you turn your problems over to the Lord, like any sensible person does? Your problems aren't any bigger than anyone else's — you just think they are!"

I sat there with my mouth open. I didn't know what to say, but I had to say something. "Well," I began, "maybe you just don't know —"

"Hold it!" Ralph held up his hand. "Stop feeling sorry for yourself long enough to let me lay something on you, Gary. There was this man who was complaining bitterly . . . he thought he'd really been shafted in life. You see, he didn't have any shoes, so he was wailing all over the place. He was really bad off."

I wondered what Ralph was getting at. "So?" I said.

"Then," Ralph went on, "he saw another man . . . *who had no feet!*"

I let it soak in, then I nodded. "See what you mean," I said, feeling a little ashamed about my hard luck nagging.

"What you need to do," Ralph said then, "is to shut your mouth and quit crying and whining and grow up and be a man!" He picked up a book from his desk, the Bible, holding it high. "If you had any sense, you'd ask for help from the one source that can give it to you — Jesus Christ!"

I felt like I'd been hit with a sledgehammer. Those were the straightest words I'd ever been belted with, and I had no answer. I simply got up, retreated to my own room, and got down on my knees by the bed.

"Dear God," I prayed, "whatever it is I have to do I'll do it. My life is in your hands." I hesitated. I'd faked a lot of prayers in my time, but this one was no fraud.

"Lord," I said aloud, "I need your help if I'm going to make it. Tell me what to do . . . where to go . . . please, Lord, help me!"

I felt a little better then. I knew I hadn't grown up and become a man as Ralph said I should, just in those few minutes, but I did feel for once I'd gone to the right authority to get what I wanted. And all of a sudden I got an unaccountable urge to go to the library and find out all I could about the Heavenly Father and His Son. If I was going to be on regular speaking terms with Them, I felt I ought to get to know Them a little better.

I started reading (always a slow process for me), and I came across a bit of scripture I didn't understand: "There is therefore now no condemnation for those who are in Christ Jesus." I couldn't figure out what that meant so I went over to John Carlson, one of the fellows from the Center who was in the library.

"What does this passage mean, John?" I asked. "I get sort of lost sometimes when I read the Bible."

He looked at the verse — Romans 8:1. Then he looked up at me. "If you've done something wrong, Gary, and you've asked Jesus to forgive you, then you don't need to condemn yourself any more. The Spirit of life in Jesus sets you free."

I thought about that for a moment, then said, "Thanks, John — thanks a lot!" And I went back to the table where I'd been studying. I felt better. I'd never really considered this whole situation prior to that afternoon.

The Lord Jesus Christ, with His infinite power to purify the soul and forgive us our sins, could free me from the self-condemnation that had been so much a part of my life. It felt really great to know I didn't have to condemn myself any more!

It gave me a sense of freedom I'd never felt before, and I closed the beautiful Book and put it back on the shelf, happier than I'd been within the limited reaches of my memory. I walked out on the street, down to the corner, and I was just standing there, my mind whirling with this new-found knowledge, when something else happened that had never happened before.

I felt a mighty explosion within, a welling up of feeling that eludes explanation in words. It was like all the years of frustration and fear and foul-up were being pushed right out of my body by a new spring of fresh water that was bubbling up inside me. I began crying, right there on that street corner, but this time — and for the first time I could ever recall — these were tears of joy. I didn't even see the cars passing by. I didn't see anything except a new light that seemed to surround me on all sides.

Surprised, even a little bit frightened, I put my hand on my heart, and when I did, I felt the forbidden pack of cigarettes I'd stowed away there in my shirt pocket earlier in the day. Automatically, out of habit, I fished one out and started to light it. But before the match could do its work, my tongue tasted the repulsive gall of the tobacco, and I jerked the weed out of my mouth and threw it to the concrete beneath my feet. Quickly, the pack followed, and I ground the entire mess into the walkway with shuffling feet. I shook my head. That was the first time I had ever, of my own volition, rid myself of perfectly good cigarettes; always before somebody had asked me for them, or simply confiscated them. I knew, without really putting it into words at the time, that I had finally put on the full armor of God.

"Thank you, Jesus!" I murmured. "Thank you, Lord! Praise God — I'm saved!"

I was so excited it was difficult to maintain self-control. All the years of hell and hopelessness were abruptly washed away when the peace of the Lord suddenly settled on me at that street corner. The prison, the dungeon I had locked my life in all those years, was suddenly transformed into a new, open temple of God. The old man I had become was free, now a new man in the Lord.

I had truly been born again, and I knew it. I had invited Jesus to become the Lord of my life. No more pretense. No more straddling the fence. I was willing to follow the Lord now, no matter where He went, no matter where He led me. I was so happy I couldn't stand still, so I headed toward a nearby park, and by the time I got there, I was jumping and leaping for joy. Christ was mine!

There I was on the peaceful grass of the park, looking at the birds soaring through the air and knowing I, too, could now soar in spirit wherever I wished, with Jesus at my side. I started talking to some dogs that were playing on the lawn, and laughing at their antics, just bubbling over with the new wine of the Spirit.

The hours and hours of study of the Bible that I'd spent, like a man of the soil planting his seeds for the harvest that would come later, became a treasure for me to reap now. I recalled the time when Peter and John were going to the temple at the hour of prayer, and a man lame since birth was at the temple gate, asking for alms.

And Peter told him, "Silver and gold have I none; but such as I have I give thee: In the name of Jesus Christ of Nazareth rise up and walk." And the man did. (Acts 3:1-10)

They didn't feed his habit; they didn't even give him money to buy food; they watched him be delivered from his burden, and he went with them into the temple, walking and leaping and praising God.

And here I was doing the same thing all over again. I, too, had been lame since birth. After all those years of sin and degradation, I had risen up to walk in the name of Jesus Christ.

When I went back to the Center I could hardly contain myself. "I've been saved — I am born again!" I hollered when I got inside the doorway.

From the expressions on their faces, I could tell some of the fellows who'd known me for quite a while were wondering if I'd gone off the deep end again.

It was an effort to hold down my enthusiasm, but I knew I had to get my serious message across to them. "Jesus came into my life this afternoon," I said to them. "The old life is gone — gone forever. I have fully accepted the Lord Jesus Christ."

"Well, *Praise God!*" It was my old friend, Ralph Coker, and he knew it was for real.

Chapter Sixteen

The freedom I felt in my new life defied description. In all the years I'd been in and out of Teen Challenge Centers and other rehabilitation units, I'd never really believed that a person could be "born again" in accepting the Lord Jesus Christ as his personal savior. Now, I believed: it had happened to me.

For the first time in my life, I didn't have anything to run away from. While I could not simply ignore a past filled with problems, I no longer felt as if those problems had the power to rise up and confront me again. I was fully confident that with Jesus at my side, I could face each new day without the gnawing fear of some incident triggering another fall by the wayside.

I took counsel from my good friend, Ralph Coker, who helped me get it all into proper perspective. "Why did I have to waste so much of my life before finding the Savior?" I asked him one day. "Why did I have to go through years and years of alcohol, drugs, jail, mental institutions, the whole bit? Why, Ralph?"

He answered me slowly, carefully. "Gary," he said, "the Lord's will isn't always easy to understand. But that's what it's all about. You could have chosen Him anytime — you certainly received enough invitations. But you had to hit bottom and *know* it was the bottom, and realize you couldn't make it without Him. And someday the Lord will be able to use every bit of what you went through. I do believe that's His will for you."

I thought it over, but it still wasn't clear. "I still don't see why He couldn't have saved me a whole lot sooner," I complained. "I don't mean to be unholy, but — well, I've been to the edge of hell and back. Why?''

Again, Ralph took his time in answering. "Tell me some-thing, Gary,'' he spoke quietly. "If you hadn't been there and back how could you relate to some other poor soul — say a drug addict who's looking for salvation but doesn't know how to find it — how could you relate to him, without having been there yourself?''

I began to see the light. I remembered something I'd picked up in one of our Bible study lessons. "God moves in mysterious ways, His wonders to perform,'' I quoted.

"You've got it,'' Ralph said. "Amen!''

The people around me at Teen Challenge in Anaheim were truly an inspiration, and our daily worship became far more meaningful to me than ever before. I had so many things to be thankful to God for . . . among them men like Bill Minor, who'd brought me there on faith; Dave Wilkerson, who'd originated Teen Challenge and had done so much to keep it moving forward; George Wakeling, whose dedication to the guiding principles of Teen Challenge was a revelation in itself.

I knew that warnings were still coming in from out of my past, but I didn't care. While I couldn't blame them for feeling as they did, I only wished they could see the new me, saved by the grace of God. And I found great personal joy in every oppor-tunity to witness to the glory of salvation through Jesus Christ.

"Here's a book you might find helpful,'' Ralph Coker said to me one day. "It's by Watchman Nee called *The Normal Chris-tian Life,* and it helps set a pattern for living in Christ.''

I accepted it gratefully and began to dig in but it was slow going. The miracle of salvation hadn't included any sudden new ability to read. I still had the old handicap of lack of fundamental education, but I gave it my best effort, and I began to learn things I'd never before thought about.

Our ministry at the Teen Challenge Center in Anaheim, that summer of 1969, brought a constant stream of young people, seeking answers to their problems. For the first time, the title of the organization took on real meaning for me. It was, indeed, a fantastic challenge to seek ways to remold distorted lives, and as Ralph had told me, I was able to relate to the addict, the alcoholic, the misguided teenager or adult in a far more realistic way, because I'd traveled the same road myself. I knew where it was at.

One night I was assigned to remain at the Center while most of the fellows went to a tent meeting. Earlier, I'd had a telephone call from a girl I'd met several years before when she was fourteen years old, and I'd suggested she go to that meeting. It wasn't unusual — voices from the past cropped up frequently enough in my life, and I forgot about the call.

I was busy digging into my book, trying to come up with the proper understanding of the bigger words, when in walked a young lady whom I immediately identified as a "cruiser." She was mini-skirted, heavy with makeup, and wearing high heels with hair piled high to match. Yet, aside from the haunted look that told me this girl's pathway had been a rocky one, there seemed to be something vaguely familiar about her. I stared at her for a moment, breathing a silent prayer to God to give me the strength and inspiration to lead her to better ways.

"Hi!" she said to me. "Remember me?"

I searched my memory, recalling the voice on the phone. "You're not — you couldn't be — Nanell Jones?"

"One and the same!" she announced.

"But you're — you must be Nanell's older sister!"

"I'm Nanell," she insisted. "Surprised that I've grown up?"

I was, indeed! This was not the same sweet little girl I'd met before. This was a hard-scoring doll off the streets, and I suddenly realized I faced the awesome responsibility of trying to help this mixed-up young lady find the answers to her problems. It would be no easy assignment.

I decided to level with her; perhaps if she knew some details of my own background, she would know I understood what was going on with her.

"I'm a different Gary Fisher now," I said. "You may not know it, but I had a reputation of being not only a drug addict and an alcoholic, but also the worst good-for-nothing backslider ever to walk through the doors of Teen Challenge."

Her lips curled into a reluctant smile, a good sign, "I've chalked up some pretty good licks myself. I've even tried suicide several times — the last one just a month ago.''

I nodded, deciding not to bring up that side of my own past. But she'd come for help. What should I do? How could I show her the love of God, the power of Jesus Christ to set her straight?

"Nanell," I said, "let me tell you something. I know you have a problem, probably with drugs, or you wouldn't be here. Right?"

She tossed her head. "Oh, maybe," she said, and I knew I'd started off wrong. But I plunged on, hoping I could convey a message that would be helpful.

"You know, we have a little saying here," I continued, "that sort of wraps up the whole drug problem in a few words. Like to hear it?"

She shrugged. "Why not?" I had the feeling this girl was quietly sneering at me, underneath, but I didn't know what to do about it.

"It goes like this," I said. "Satan rides a snowy white horse, and his name is Junkie. He has a partner named Suicide, and a following of three called L-S-D . . . Lucifer, Satan and the Devil. His army is full of red devils, yellow jackets, and many more fiends, and they're all having a grassy experience, heading for a smoky ending. How about that?"

I was blowing it and I knew it. "The answer to our problems," I went on, "is in Jesus Christ. Did you know He died for our sins?"

"Oh, sure." Again, that casual flippancy. And then, "I was over at the tent meeting you told me about, but I didn't dig it much. You doing anything after you're through here?"

What was the matter? What was I doing wrong? Here was this tripped-out girl, looking for help, and I wasn't getting through to her.

"I'll be on duty all night," I said, "so I can help anyone who might come in."

She nodded, just sitting there looking at me, and I breathed another prayer. "Dear Lord," I thought, "if it be thy will, help me to reach out and touch this poor soul who needs help. Give me the words, give me the strength to bring her to You. Help me, Lord."

I sat there waiting, but I suddenly realized I couldn't expect the good Lord to strike me with superb wisdom just any old time I wanted it. I'd have to do my part, too. "Thank you, Jesus!" I thought. "Thank you!"

I held up my book. "Got a real good book here," I said. "It's called *The Normal Christian Life.* Got a lot of good stuff in it."

Again she nodded, not saying anything. I could have gone on and told her how I needed this direction for my own footsteps, how it was like walking through molasses — a constant struggle to determine what the words in the book were, and trying to put them together for the meaning they held. But I didn't. Our conversation was becoming painfully scanty. There had to be some way to reach out to her, for beneath the makeup and the outward flamboyant appearance, I could sense the same fears and frustrations and defiance that had marked my own life in earlier days. There had to be some way for me to bring her to the Lord.

Sitting there in the big chair in the Teen Challenge office, her tiny figure almost lost in it, she seemed to be reaching out for help I wasn't giving her. So I breathed another silent prayer — "Lord, please show me the way."

And then the words began flowing. "Nanell," I said, "do you know that you'd never have come to Teen Challenge if the Lord hadn't sent you? That's the way He works. He brought me to Teen Challenge, too, but it took a long time for me to get on the right path." I paused, hoping I was getting a message across. "It's different with each one," I said. "It can happen to you right now."

She just sat there looking at me, and I was afraid I'd mess it up.

"It's written in the Scriptures," I went on. "If any man be in Christ, he is a new creature — old things are passed away. Behold, all things are become new!" I couldn't remember exactly where that came from, but I took a shot at it anyway. "That's in Second Corinthians."

Still no answer, no comment from Nanell Jones. So I picked it up again. "And that means women, too, where it says 'If any man be in Christ,' " I said. "It means all of us."

She nodded. Was I getting through to her? " 'Believe on the Lord Jesus Christ,' " I quoted, " 'and thou shalt be saved.' That's from the book of Acts.''

"You seem to know a lot of Bible verses," Nanell said. The words were barely above a whisper.

"It's the greatest book ever written," I told her warmly. "It's all there — all the answers to life and all the problems any of us ever have.''

My young lady guest nodded. I reached back into my memory to come up with another verse. " 'If we confess our sins, He is faithful and just to forgive us our sins, and to cleanse us from all unrighteousness,' " I said. "That's from the Book of John — or maybe it's First John. Anyway, that's how Jesus works.''

I waited, but no sound from Nanell. So I tried another approach. "All you have to do is confess with your mouth and believe in your heart that Jesus Christ was resurrected from the dead, and you will be saved," I said quietly. "Do you believe, Nanell?''

Again a barely perceptible nod. Then, without warning, one of the fellows at the Center rushed in, took a look at Nanell sitting there dejectedly in the big chair, and came up with what he apparently thought was a big idea.

"Oh, Gary!" he said, "let's cast out all the demons from her — she's of the devil!''

I was afraid at that instant that he'd undone anything good that might have been started. "Hey, that door swings both ways, brother," I told him. "Now you split, and let the Lord handle this situation. Can't you see He's already working in her?''

The other guy looked at me for a moment, then turned and walked out, closing the door behind him. And at that instant, tears began flowing down Nanell's cheeks, so I knew the Lord had touched her heart. The Holy Spirit had fallen on her, and I wondered what I should do now.

"Please, God," I prayed silently, "help me bring her to Christ!''

There were great sobs wracking her body now, and I felt I

should offer her a reassuring hand — yet, I was afraid she'd get the wrong idea, so I just sat there.

"Jesus loves you, Nanell," I said softly. "He'll forgive all your sins."

She continued to sob and her hair fell down around her face and the tears began to wash away her makeup. "Praise God!" I said then. "Come into her heart, dear Jesus!"

With the tears still streaming, Nanell suddenly got up from the chair, and without a word, opened the door and ran out. My own heart sank. Despite my prayers and my faith in the Lord, I'd blown it. With heavy feet, I went outside, and to my amazement, she was still there, standing at the curb, reaching into her purse and throwing pills and cigarettes and other things I couldn't identify into the gutter!

I just stood there with my mouth open, and when she'd carefully gone through her purse and thrown away everything she wanted to be rid of, she turned to me with a triumphant smile beaming through the tears. "I'm never going to touch that stuff again as long as I live!" she declared.

"God bless you!" I said. "Praise the Lord!"

It was the most graphic demonstration of the power of God I'd yet seen, for I could feel the presence of the Holy Spirit surrounding us. God had touched Nanell that night and put her on a real high. I continued to talk with her briefly, and finally dared to do what I hadn't done before — I held out my hand for her to clasp.

"Thank you, Gary!" she said softly.

"Thank you, Jesus!" I corrected her. "He's the one who did it!"

She looked up into the night. "Thank you, Jesus!" she murmured, and my heart sang.

I went back to the office, but I couldn't settle down. The exhilaration of the evening's experience had me soaring in spirit as I'd never soared before. Then, after a half an hour or so, the telephone rang.

"Gary, this is Nanell," a sweet voice told me, after I'd identified myself. "I just wanted you to know — I've never been so excited! I've never been so happy!"

"Thank God!" I said fervently. "Thank you, Jesus!"

"I just praise God because He's really touched my life!" Nanell went on. "I — wanted you to know!"

"The Lord performs all sorts of miracles," I told her then. "All we have to do is believe in Him."

"I do, Gary! Oh, I do!" Her voice was strong now, full of new life. "I'll — see you tomorrow!"

"Great!" I said. "Goodnight — and God bless you, Nanell."

The next morning at eight, when I opened the door to the Center as was my custom, there, sitting on the front steps, was Nanell. And that's the way it was from then on — every day she would come down to the Teen Challenge Center and sit and wait for the front door to open so she could join us in praising the Lord with our daily devotions.

It didn't take me long to learn she was an excellent reader, and knowing that she shared with me the need for Christian guidance, I again showed her my book — *The Normal Christian Life*. And without embarrassment, I explained my problem.

"I wondered if maybe you could read it out loud to me," I suggested.

"Sure," she said. "Let's go down to the park."

So each day we'd walk over to the nearby park, and she would read a chapter of the book to me. It taught us both a great deal. It taught us that every day is the same — every day, no matter how you feel, you have to walk by faith. You have to learn to grasp the fullness of the joy of the Lord, to face up to this old world just the way it is. but with confidence that God is on your side.

It wasn't all roses; there were occasional thorns, too. One day Nanell arrived at the Center and one of our more ardent crusaders came in and started telling her off.

"If you don't take off all that makeup and those earrings," he said, "and get rid of those eyelashes and short skirts, you're going straight to hell!"

This was the wrong thing to say to Nanell, and I knew it, but before I could stop her, she ran out of the building and jumped into her car. I ran after her, a prayer in my heart.

"Please, God!" I breathed. "Don't let it happen!" I was well aware of the delicate thread of faith holding her together, and I was desperately fearful that my well-intentioned friend had broken it.

I knocked on the window of her car, before she could get it started. "Nanell! Please!"

She unlocked the door, tears coursing down her cheeks. But she made no sound. She just sat there as I got in beside her.

"Nanell," I said, "don't listen to him. He — means well, but he doesn't realize. . ." I was groping for the right words. "Listen to the Holy Spirit, Nanell," I went on. "Let the Holy Spirit talk to you and convict you. Then you'll know what to do."

A bright smile gradually replaced the tears as she turned to me. "Thank you, Gary," she said. "I will!"

Slowly, a change began to take place, as Nanell continued her daily visits to our Teen Challenge Center. The false eyelashes disappeared. Then the heavy makeup began to diminish, revealing a rosy-cheeked complexion that was far more attractive than all the cosmetics in the world. The short skirts were lengthened. Our little rebel, Nanell, was coming around, becoming a real lady, and we joined in thanking the Holy Spirit for this exciting transformation.

Nanell and I began visiting schools together, giving our testimony to the Lord, and this led to dating. We continued to go to the park for reading sessions, delving into the eternal truth of the Bible, after we'd finished *The Normal Christian Life.*

There came a special day at the beach for Nanell and me when the promise was made. Nanell Jones would someday become Mrs. Gary Fisher.

But that meant some additional problems, too. We loved each other in the Lord, but we also loved each other for ourselves, and we knew the Lord wanted us to do right in His sight. The temptations were real and heavy. So knowing we needed help, we turned to the always-available source, and prayed to God for guidance. He spoke to both of us then and there. He told us to get Nanell's mother and ask her to ride along with us on our various missions.

"Mom, would you ride along with us whenever we're out together?" Nanell asked that night.

"We don't want to do anything wrong, and we feel that's the best plan," I explained.

And that began a period of fourteen months with "Mom" riding along with us. At first, the suggestion just about blew her mind, understandably, but when she realized just how serious we were in wanting to do right, she was with us all the way. Not only that, Christ really touched Nanell's mom's life, filling her with the joy of the Lord, as we journeyed here and there to give our testimony. She was wonderful company for us, and we both loved her for it.

But our problems hadn't ended. The road ahead, had we only known it, was still strewn with stoppers of one kind or another. Even though we were stepping out on faith, the past would not always let us alone.

Nanell and I were sitting in the car by ourselves one day after witnessing to people in the nearby park and telling them about Jesus. Suddenly, she began having one of her all-too-frequent flashbacks — the result of the innumerable acid trips she'd taken before getting into even heavier drugs. My face began melting, right before her eyes, and she started screaming in terror.

Frightened beyond belief, I sat there petrified. What could I do? As though a demon had possessed her, this sweet girl I was going to marry was pushing at me, her voice an unintelligible shriek, her eyes mirroring the sheer horror my being there created in her distorted mind.

What, in the name of God, could I do?

Chapter Seventeen

If Nanell was frightened out of her wits by the illusion her past drug experience was producing, I was stunned senseless by the suddenness with which she had changed. At first I thought she was putting me on, but only for a moment; the look of panic wrenching her face was all too real. I'd delved deep into the Word, but I couldn't recall having found the answer to this problem, because I'd never anticipated one like this.

Then, as though in response to my unspoken prayer, a Bible verse came to me: "I can do all things through Christ which strengtheneth me." I had no choice; I had to act, to use the aid at hand.

Grasping Nanell's terror-stricken face in both my hands, I spoke aloud. "In the name of Jesus, dear God, help her!"

For a split-second, Nanell's eyes held onto the stark shock of abject fear. Then, as suddenly as her fright had begun, her face softened, she relaxed, and I knew God had answered my desperate prayer. He had reached out to touch her, and I took my own hands from her face, amazed at the alteration.

"Thank you, Lord!" I said fervently. "Thank you, Jesus!"

Nanell bowed her head. "Amen!" she said reverently.

And from that day on there were no more flashbacks — a fact we both consider to be a miracle. For she had suffered, as I had, some horrible experiences because of her drug habit.

When she was living in sin and out on the streets, some hippies picked her up and turned her on with some strong acid. Then they coaxed her into a room where they kept a pet garden snake. The snake, of course, was harmless, but being on a heavy acid trip in a room with a snake was an experience that could well have marked her for life. It was a long time after that trip before Nanell was normal. The hippies, having had their fun, called her mother, then left her on a street corner for the family to pick up.

Nanell had been gone from her family for a couple of weeks, and of course they were most thankful to get her home, for it was a special occasion: It was her sixteenth birthday, and her mother's gift to her was a lovely white Bible.

By using the same technique of pretense which I had perfected, she had cut the inside out of another Bible she carried, to make a place where she could stash her drugs without anyone suspecting. She led a rough life for quite some time, and it terminated only when she came to Teen Challenge and found Jesus Christ. Each day we both took the time to praise the Lord for His love in showing us the way.

I continued working at Teen Challenge, earning five dollars a week, but life was good, and I would take Nanell out to dinner once a week, using half my salary for that special event. The other half I'd use for another good purpose, perhaps best illustrated by an incident that occurred not long after we became engaged.

As I often did, I went to Nanell's folks' mobile home for dinner, and left my coat on the divan while I went to the bathroom. Admiring the coat, Percy — Nanell's father — looked it over, and then told her mother that I must be loaded with money, because the label said the coat was imported from England.

Imported it may have been, but like all my clothes, it came straight from the Salvation Army Store, where I took my remaining $2.50 after buying dinner for Nanell and myself on our night out. I had just bought the coat that same day.

Randy Burks, the supervisor at Teen Challenge and my roommate, had much the same experience. "Say, Gary," he remarked one day, "you've got the finest wardrobe in town. How do you do it?"

So from that time on, Randy, too, was able to obtain shirts

and socks and shoes and other clothing the same way I did . . . a real blessing at a time when it was sorely needed.

Getting back to Nanell's parents, I cannot say enough about the way they helped me at a time when I needed all the assistance I could get. Nanell's dad was a wonderful, hard-working man who wanted the best for his children. He and Louise, her mother, opened their home to me during the time Nanell and I were going together, making their home mine, and feeding me dinners for more than a year. Again, this was a blessing at a time when it was needed most.

Nanell's father especially enjoyed passing out tracts to young people and he delighted in telling them how his daughter had been saved, with the Lord setting her free from drugs. He would put Christian literature in places where he knew the kids would hang out and go to get loaded. His hope that they'd have the same wonderful experience of finding Jesus as his daughter had was often fulfilled.

Nanell's sister, Linda, and her brother, Dave, were also always encouraging me, along with Linda's boyfriend, Steve. To both Nanell and me they were of immeasurable help, because they were on our side — they cared!

* * * *

I discovered in reading my Bible that Jesus did not always win an immediate victory. When He directed the steps of men to the difficult path they must take, some "went back, and walked no more with Him." He won some, He lost some. But He knew how to face the mountains of defeat and to draw from those same mountains a strength of character and purpose that would not be denied.

It was that way for us at the Teen Challenge Center, as time after time the Holy Spirit did indeed descend and transform someone who sought aid and guidance through us. It was a thrilling time — soul-stirring because of the joy Christ brought to our hearts when we saw these miracles of transfiguration, thanks to Him.

We learned many lessons, of course. We knew from bitter experience that the drug addict needs to get out in the open air and find a new way for himself — that's why Christ is the answer. The Bible is what gives him a new mind, and we were simply tools in God's hands to bring about the needed change.

Every drug addict who kicks his habit in a hospital, as I did on repeated occasions, can endure the physical anguish of severe bodily pain, but he can't turn off his mind . . . he keeps on thinking about the craving for drugs that afflicts him, and the result is almost invariably a regression to the same old habits.

That's why faith in God is so important. He helps us think about the positive things, the good things, the great things that Jesus did and continues to do through us, His servants. At Teen Challenge we came to realize that we never have sufficient strength within ourselves, but with Christ at our side, we could conquer every obstacle.

It seemed it could go on forever, but our preparations for a life's work of serving the Lord finally began to pay the worth-while dividends we all hoped for. The house we were staying in — our Center — was a very large, old, Spanish-style structure, and the rent was high. We had trouble getting support for our work, and this we accepted as God's will. He was pushing us on to other things, for the fullness of time had come, and God had done His work in each of our lives. It was now time for each one of us to branch out into our own ministries.

Bill Minor decided to leave Teen Challenge and start a Hot Line and at the same time Ralph Wilkerson wanted to start a 24-hour Hot Line at Melodyland, near Disneyland in Anaheim. George Patton and Don Madison each wanted to start a program of their own to help drifting drug addicts. Teen Challenge, too, wanted to continue its work, so there were difficult choices to be made.

After hours of prayer, I decided to go along with Ralph Wilkerson and Bill Minor to the Hot Line at Melodyland. Randy Burks was offered positions by all the others, but he chose to go with George Patton, and the two of them started the Trans-formation House. So the split was complete. There were new directions for all.

It wasn't easy to start the Hot Line, but we were a dedicated group of individuals, all of us looking constantly to the Lord for help, and slowly it began to work. We got an apartment to house the operation and both Nanell and I took different shifts on the Hot Line to keep it open all night long as a refuge for the lost, confused youngsters who'd gotten strung out on drugs and didn't know which way to turn. And because we'd been there ourselves, we could relate to their problems, making it easier to turn them in a different direction.

I would go on the Line one night, and stay till the following night. Then Ralph Coker, my old friend, would take his turn. Bill Minor — to whom I shall always be indebted for coming to my rescue when I and everyone else had thrown in the towel — decided he'd like to move on to another type of ministry, so Don Musgraves took over the Hot Line, and the Lord really started to multiply it. We'd get down on our knees and pray every single day, praising God and thanking Him for our success.

We started a choir, a radio program, and the Hot Line grew more and more, as we expanded our ministry.

We were busy day and night. As Outreach Director I assumed responsibility for getting two messages across to the thousands of young people in the Orange County schools: the dangers of drugs and alcohol, and the saving power of the Lord. Nanell, I, and two or three others went to so many schools (more than 300), we began to think we, too, were still in school.

We'd report to a school at 8:00 in the morning, usually for an assembly of all the students, and I'd tell them how the Melody-land Hot Line program got started. Then Nanell and other girls would testify about all they'd undergone and how their lives had been changed. We'd all testify to the greatness of God in rehabilitating our existence.

Then, often until 3:00 in the afternoon, we'd visit individual classes to answer questions about drugs and to verify how the Lord had set us free. There were times when kids would line up for a block just to talk to us. We'd feel like we were turning into pills ourselves before we got through the day. Our visits to schools would go on three or four days a week, interspersed with presentations at various service clubs — Kiwanis, Rotary, Optimist, Lions — plus PTA and other organizations.

Melodyland began to be flooded to overflowing with young

people showing up to hear more of this unique message that we told them was the answer to whatever problems they'd been facing. Often we found the parents of those we talked to were guilty of neglect, if not outright rejection. They would send their children to us along with checks to cover any cost, in effect washing their hands of responsibilities they should have shouldered long ago.

Our program received national recognition for its effectiveness. Not only did it merit the highly-coveted Disneyland Community Service Award (repeated several times in later years), but it was also covered extensively in *Look* magazine, still a popular national publication in 1969. We've been told since that much of what happened would never have come about without the dedication to the service of the Lord that Nanell and I and those helping us were happy to express.

Nanell and I were still going together, still taking her mother everywhere we went. There were more and more opportunities to preach, and one of God's greatest blessings came when I was licensed as a minister, then ordained. The call was now clearer than ever. I was truly a minister of the Lord, and I wanted to preach the gospel at every opportunity.

But it wasn't all that easy. I wanted to be able to read and write, too — to be able to prepare my sermons for the glory of God. So I went back to a familiar spot — the library — and I went into a section filled with great big books. It was about time I dug in and really made something of myself.

About that time, I heard a voice I'd heard before, but hadn't always heeded. This time I listened, knowing the voice could be heard at that time and place by me alone.

"Son," the voice said, "what are you doing there among all those big books?"

I gulped. How could I answer the Lord? "Well," I said aloud, "I want to become real heavy in Your ministry — like Bob Mumford and Dick Mills. I want to get real deep into the Word. I want to make it for You!"

"You're going at it backwards," the voice said to me then. "You don't even know how to read the Word yet." I hung my head, for this was true. I had a terribly long way to go.

"Go over into the children's section," was the next advice I heard.

So I went over there and got into the nursery rhymes and the fairy tales, and I began to relate the characters and events to the Word. I ran into Jack and the Bean Stalk, and the Lord said, "I am the vine and you are the branches."

"Wow!" I said. "That's heavy, Lord!"

I pulled out Little Red Riding Hood, and suddenly she became Righteous Red, for the red cape she wore on the way to her grandma's pad stood for the blood of Jesus Christ.

I met the Gingerbread Man, and he became the gingerbread junkie, always running from God, unwilling to share his love with anyone else. I recalled that Jesus said, "I am the bread of life, and if I am the bread of life, so are you, and you should share your bread with one another. Break your bread with one another." I was simply overwhelmed.

"Wow!" I said again. "This is really heavy!"

Then I found Tom Thumb, and the same voice which guided me to the children's section of the library told me to relate his story to the 23rd Psalm — "The Lord is my shepherd, I shall not want. . ." I knew I had found my own way to express the message of truth and light . . . the message of the Heavenly Father and His Son, Jesus Christ.

God didn't stop there, either. He guided me to a little ranch, with three acres of land, and ducks and chickens all over the place, available for $20 a week. It was a heaven-sent blessing, for I took my Webster's dictionary and a Moody Bible book, and I started reading the Word of God as never before. The Holy Spirit took over and taught me how to read, and I began preaching to my ducks and chickens.

I preached to the trees, to anything that got in my way. I preached to the mirror, to the wall, to a tape recorder. And relating those simple nursery rhymes and fairy tales and some of the familiar biblical stories to the Word of God, I was surprised at the ease with which I could drive home the points I wanted to make, even though they weren't being made at those moments to a very meaningful audience.

For some time I was almost a hermit, I was so absorbed in

learning to give God's message. There was a little shack on the ranch which I used as a study room, and I smiled to recall that trailers and shacks had played a significant role in my life.

It was a time of sober reflection, and the more I studied, the more convinced I was this was the calling to which I wanted to dedicate my life. I finally realized if you want to do something badly enough, you can do it. You just have to want it strongly enough, plus you have to place the whole matter in the hands of God, with faith that He will deliver if it is His will.

* * * *

It was time, I knew, for Nanell and me to be married, for we had waited faithfully for a long time. That day, May 2, 1970, was a day I'll never forget, standing there before the altar, with Don Musgraves ready to perform the ceremony and my beautiful bride walking slowly down the aisle on her father's arm. She looked like an angel, and I mean a real live angel! A surge of happiness flooded through me, because the Lord and I had finally turned things around to where I was doing something that was right and good and acceptable in His eyes.

I'd been on the right path for some time, of course, but, in a sense, this was the final confirmation that a new Gary Fisher had replaced the old one. I had finally sought first the Kingdom of God and His Righteousness, and many good things were being added unto me. My wrongs were becoming rights. I wasn't walking backward anymore. I had begun to walk forward, and the old world I had endured was only a memory.

Nanell came up to me and I looked into her lovely eyes and realized that God had given me the desire of my heart. She was my rib, come home, and I breathed a prayer: "Thank you, Jesus!"

After we repeated the vows of the ceremony and turned to go back up the aisle, we were hurrying so fast that Nanell got her foot caught in the hoop of her wedding gown — hooked again! It cracked everyone up, of course, because she couldn't move — she couldn't walk. But everyone around her helped get her foot undone, and by the time we got outside after the photo-taking session, our friends — a lot of them youngsters — threw so much rice at us, it almost knocked us over. We literally needed the full armor of God for protection. And as we left the chapel, tin cans rattling behind us, it was the end and the beginning.

For me, it was the end of a life that had taken me through the torments of hell. The abuse — both from others and self-inflicted — I had seen for twenty-nine years was unbelievable . . . parental neglect, houses for children without parents, alcoholism, drug addiction, mental suffering, homosexuality, back alley brawls, jails . . . I'd seen them all and more.

For Nanell, it was likewise a complete reversal. Her years of troubles were fortunately fewer, but here was a girl who had taken two hundred LSD trips . . . who had sliced her wrists three times in desperate attempts to get away from her problems . . . who found that Juvenile Hall and talking with psychiatrists did not provide any answers . . . a girl who had gone through things that really can't be talked about. Nothing helped until she found the Lord.

That God could take two lives so wrecked and backslidden as ours, renew them inside out, and join them in marriage and give them new life in His service was nothing short of a miracle. And as we drove along following the wedding, the magnitude of our blessings hit me so hard I started to cry, praising God for what He had done in our behalf.

And although we didn't really realize it at the time, this marriage was remarkably meaningful to those around us. Here were two confirmed drug addicts who'd been about as far down as the human spirit can get; both of us had been rehabilitated through the Teen Challenge program; both of us had accepted Christ into our hearts and lives; both of us had worked hard to bring others to Christ, and with His help we had been eminently successful.

We went north to Big Sur and Three Rivers for our honeymoon, returning to the little ranch two weeks later. Our work together for the Hot Line at Melodyland continued. We went to schools, held PTA meetings and programs and ministered in every way we could. I would preach at every available opportunity, and the knowledge that God was using me as an instrument to reach those in need was a heavy responsibility indeed, but one I happily shouldered, knowing I had Nanell at my side and the saving power of Jesus Christ to carry us through.

Then there came a day I'd been dreading. I was asked to perform a marriage ceremony for the first time, and recalling how I'd felt at my own wedding, I wasn't sure I could do it.

"What if I blow it?" I asked Nanell.

She looked at me with those sparkling eyes and smiled. "You won't blow it," she said quietly. "Just remember Who's on your side — Who's really joining the bride and groom together. With Him on your side, how could you blow it?"

She was right, and I knew it. But just the same, I figured a little practice wouldn't hurt anything at all. So I took our two dogs and put them in the bedroom and closed the door. I married them three times before I was satisfied I could properly recite the necessary vows.

That first wedding went off without a hitch. I haven't the foggiest notion of how many people were there, nor do I know whether it was mine or the groom's knees that were knocking the loudest. I do know, however, that I simply put my trust in God, and, as usual, He came through. "Ask and you shall receive," He says. It works.

The first funeral I ever officiated at was for Nanell's grandmother, and once again, I resorted to rehearsal time. I had the fullest trust in the Lord, but I knew from experience that He expected me to do my part, too. This time it just happened that our pet parakeet, Jacob, passed on at about the same time as Grandmother. So I performed a full funeral for Jacob, and when the real rites came a short time later, I was ready for God's blessing in presenting His comforting words to those who were bereaved.

The bounty of God's blessings began not long after we were married. We were continuing to work with the Melodyland drug prevention program and living on our little ranch, when a lovely lady named Lori Ellis decided to give us a 1960 Nash station wagon. It resulted in a real drive for us to do something more for the Lord, because it enabled us to go into a separate part-time ministry — something that just hadn't been possible before.

One night after I'd preached at one of the Hot Line meetings at Melodyland, a charming little lady came marching up to me. She looked like a real saint of God — she just seemed to glow all over, radiant with love. A friend introduced her as "Mom" Taylor.

"Gary, I'd like you to come to my house and minister to the young people I have there," she said. "They need someone like you — someone who can talk their language and touch their hearts. Will you do it?"

I hesitated. Was this the opportunity I had waited for? Was my ministry, indeed, to be expanded?

I held out my hand to this gentle woman with the starry smile. "I'll be there," I said. "Just tell me when and where!"

Chapter Eighteen

In my mind I went over the sermons I'd preached to the chickens and the ducks at the ranch, but since they'd paid about as much attention to one message as another they weren't much help in deciding what to talk about when I went to Mom Taylor's place. So I talked to God about it — I prayed for guidance and help — and the thought came to me to make use of one of the nursery rhymes I'd run into, one that related to my own life.

"But nobody will listen," I protested.

"You preach it, Gary," God seemed to say, "and I'll see that they listen."

And then He reminded me of a portion of Scripture that explained why this type of message gets the point across. "But God hath chosen the foolish things of the world to confound the wise; and God hath chosen the weak things of the world to confound the things which are mighty." (I Cor. 1:27)

It was an informal situation, right in the front room of the Taylor home, with kids sitting around on couches and chairs waiting to hear what I had to say.

I decided to lay it on the line, right at the start. "How many of you ever heard of Humpty Dumpty?" I asked, and of course they grinned and nodded. This was something they could readily understand.

"This cat, Humpty," I went on, "sat on a wall, but he was a kind of restless dude, always figuring things were better on the other side, so he fiddled around and finally fell off.

"You know what that did to him — all the king's horses and all the king's men couldn't get it together again for old Humpty."

I paused and looked around the room; to my surprise, the simple lead-in had really captured the attention of these kids. "Thank you, Jesus," I prayed to myself. "Well," I went on, "I was Humpty Dumpty, sitting on that wall. I fell off and broke into pieces because I got on the whole booze and drug kick." I went on to explain that I'd tried them all, and then I told them the results of what I'd done.

"The problem with me was," I said, "not a one or even *all* of the king's men could put this Humpty Dumpty back together again. None of the hospitals I was in, none of the jails, none of the mental institutions, with their psychiatrists and shock treatments, could put me back together again.

"My Humpty Dumpty treatments just ran me out in the streets again, where I started sticking a needle in my arm. I started using morphine and heroin. I started spending sixty dollars a day, to keep myself in what I thought was filling the gap in my life, what I thought was real.

"But it wasn't. I was trying to buy peace of mind and peace in my heart, where I could sit down and righteously rest. Sixty dollars a day! But I PAY NOTHING FOR JESUS! Because He's the gift of God, and He's the only answer to our problems.

"If you're a Humpty Dumpty, like I was, and you need someone to put you back together, there's only one answer — the Lamb of God. Once you get a taste of Him, you'll never give up. It's like coming up from the grave, a whole new life!"

I looked around me, and I realized that these kids were getting the message. It was making them think. God had moved, through me, to get the Word to them.

I called for questions, knowing that the closer I could come to these kids in an informal rap session, the more chances there would be to bring them to Christ. It was exciting, an unparalleled thrill to feel the surge of God's love in that room.

Afterward, Mom Taylor came up to me and pressed a $10 bill into my hand. You can't imagine what that did to my faith, because I felt I'd truly found a ministry that could grow and grow. Which is exactly what it did — I ministered there for a long time, and I could see that God had His hand on the lives of Mom and Pop Taylor and those around them. Pop was taken to his heavenly home not too long after that, but Mom Taylor carried on, counseling and loving those wrong-way kids and helping them get straightened out.

The ministry there was blessed, and the Lord provided a larger house in Garden Grove, with a big room we could use as a chapel. Mom asked me to come and keep on preaching there, so I did, and God just filled that place. Kids were all over; they packed the whole house, everywhere. God was saving them, baptizing them in the Holy Spirit, filling them to overflowing with new lives.

Drug addicts were coming in, getting saved. Because I could talk their language, because I'd been there myself, I could get God's Word across to them. Young girls who'd turned to prostitution were saved. Young people with real bad experiences, such as homosexual involvement, parental beatings or other parent-child abuse, even some kids on pass from mental institutions would come, and God would set them free. And they'd pick up their lives, ready to make something of them now, and leave and get married and have children and become gainful citizens. What a thrill it was to see those lives straightened out, thanks to Mom Taylor's inspired and generous work. And I'm happy to say that she's still active, and that God is continuing to move in her ministry.

To cite an example of what God's saving grace can accomplish, there was Mitch, already a grown man when his worried brother, Jack Gutman, took me to see him. Mitch was oppressed by the devil, for he was convinced he had committed the unforgivable sin of blaspheming against the Holy Spirit, and that he was doomed to eternal hell. He was bitter, angry with the world. I talked with him for more than an hour, and I laid hands on him, praying to God to forgive whatever sin weighed down his life. Deliverance came as it can and does when God's hand is sought, and Mitch has returned to normalcy as a happy, productive man, secure in the love of the Lord.

Among the many persons I met during my combined ministry

at Melodyland Hot Line and at Mom Taylor's were Dan and June Duncan, sincere and interested laymen who wanted to set up a drug rehabilitation program because they saw the need. June asked me to come and talk with, or preach to, eight young people she and Dan were sheltering, so I began going there to teach those eight kids every night. It went well and June then asked me to conduct a crusade in Santa Ana.

"I'll sure give it a try," I told her, "but I'd better warn you — I've never conducted a meeting like that before by myself."

She smiled. "Let's just let the Lord worry about that," she said. "He's blessed your work up to now, so let's see what'll happen next."

So I got some messages together, and I prayed to God to see me through. I needed to pray. I was suffering severely from gout in my feet, and it was quite painful to stand on them. But at the meetings I started talking about Holy Jack and his beanstalk, and I told them about Righteous Red and her trip through the woods to Grandmother's house, and about the Three Little Pigs who were named Jude, Pete, and Rocky, and the kids started to flock in.

It was a lot like being on skid row, for the building where we held the meetings was in a pretty bad area of Santa Ana, right on the streetfront. Alcoholics and drunks would pass by, pause, listen, and often come in to hear more. I started preaching my fairy tales and nursery rhymes, and the place was so packed kids were clear back to the windows, sitting there getting the message of the Lord. There were even people standing out in the street looking in, and the power of God really took over. I had never seen anything like it. People were being touched and healed, and restored — and I knew as never before that I had nothing to do with it. It was a sovereign move of God's Spirit, and I felt empty inside, but in a good way — all hollowed out and cleansed, to be used as His vessel.

Out of that crusade, the Lord delivered 59 drug addicts from their bondage. And He left me so overjoyed and fulfilled, I would have been happy to go to Heaven right then and there. But he had something else in mind; in fact, it was nothing less than a whole new work! I couldn't believe it. He provided a church, five acres of land, four houses in which we could minister to foster children and to addicts, and even a brand new bus, which meant we could set up a full-scale drug program! My tears were tears of joy!

We called our church the Chapel of the Cross, and I became the Youth Pastor. I'd thought at first, after that crusade and its success that God was going to call me into the evangelistic ministry, but He stopped me from speculating, because what He really wanted to do was teach me some things . . . and I'm grateful that He did. In a way, it was like my having to go through all the horrible experiences of living the life of an alcoholic and an addict before I could become an effective minister of God. Now I needed to learn what went on inside the heart of a church, for it's the heart of a church — and the heart is its people — that needs to be nurtured and, sometimes, healed.

I needed to learn what it was like, the confusion you face when you go to a prayer meeting and nobody shows up, but you can go ahead and pray, just the same. I needed to find out what it was like to preach when only two or three people show up — to know what it means to go ahead and perform one's duties as a minister of the Lord, when nobody else wants to perform them. I began to realize that these were things God wanted to teach me. I had to find out what it was like to be the janitor of the church as well as its preacher.

I had to know how to carry out all the functions of a church, how to be an effective counselor with people in trouble. And I had to learn that the road to becoming a minister of God was not entirely an easy one. We did all kinds of things to keep our little chapel going. We set up a Christmas tree lot in early December, 1971, to raise funds. We had youth services on a continuing basis, and on Thursday nights were rallies where the young kids, who'd been turned onto drugs, would show up in bunches.

But the Lord blessed our obedience. He brought people from all over, and we shook our heads in wonder as the people piled in. The Chapel of the Cross and its drug program were a resounding success. It was during this time that an official of an Orange County savings and loan association, Burt Parker, came to hear me preach. Burt was a long-time resident of Buena Park, and he wrote a weekly newspaper column about events and personalities of interest in the community. He wanted to do a column on my work with addicts.

"Great!" I told him, and went on to explain how I was using nursery rhymes and fairy tales and familiar stories from the Bible, like David and Goliath, to bring the message of the gospel to our audiences.

"You know, those would make a fantastic book," Burt suggested.

I'd already thought about that, but I knew I could never do it without help. "Yeah," I said. "I wish I knew someone who could put it all together."

Burt smiled. "I think I know just the man," he said. "I'll see if I can get you two together."

And as though it were God's will, before he could set up an appointment, I happened to be at the savings and loan office in Buena Park a few days later when Burt told me he wanted me to meet someone.

"This is Bob McGrath," he said. "He's the writer I told you about. I think you two ought to talk about doing a book of your sermons."

Bob was handling public relations work for the savings and loan association, and he was also a successful free-lance writer. We arranged to get together later, to discuss putting some of those "far-out" sermons into a book. I had tape recordings of each one, and he wrote out five of them, then outlined fifteen more, and began sending the manuscript out to potential publishers.

But nothing came of it. I kept in touch with Bob, and he told me not to give up. "If doing the book of sermons was God's idea and not ours, He'll find a home for it — in His way and His time," he said.

For two years I was head over heels in the youth ministry of the Chapel of the Cross. Nanell was always by my side, propping me up when things looked bad, always ready with a helping hand and a "never-say-die" spirit that meant a lot to me when the going was rough.

During the first year of our Chapel of the Cross Christmas

tree lot when I was putting in 18-hour days to make it pay off with the extra dollars we needed so desperately for the Chapel, Nanell came up to me with some unexpected news.

"Gary, Art Linkletter called today," she said. "He wants you to call him."

I couldn't believe it. For someone as well-known as Art Linkletter — the television personality and successful business man — to call me was like another miracle. I'd written to him some time before, and he told Nanell he'd enjoyed my letter and called because he wanted to talk to me. So we made an appointment and Dan, Nanell and I went to his office in Los Angeles one morning.

Because I was so anxious to talk to Mr. Linkletter, we got to his office before the appointed time — almost an hour ahead of time, in fact — and as the minutes wore away, I became convinced it was all a hoax.

Nanell just smiled. "Where's your faith?" she asked quietly. So I sat down and thanked the good Lord again for this wonderful helpmate He'd given me.

Finally the receptionist said the magic words. "Mister Linkletter will see you now."

We walked in, to see a tall, refined gentleman who welcomed us with a reserved smile. "I was quite impressed with your letter, Gary," he said. "I'd like to hear more about your chapel's drug program."

While I talked about our efforts to rejuvenate youngsters who'd gone wrong, I noticed that Art Linkletter from time to time turned to look at Nanell. And when she talked of some of her own past problems and our current work, he seemed to hang on every word.

"I assume you know my daughter took her own life while under the influence of LSD," he said finally, after we'd covered all aspects of our program.

We nodded, uncertain what to say. "You have much to be thankful for," he said sadly to Nanell then. "Very much!'

Nanell smiled. "I know. I'm thankful to Jesus," she said. "He's the only answer."

We talked with Mr. Linkletter that morning for an hour, and

he gave us a letter of recommendation for contacting various service clubs for the financial support we needed so badly. He also gave me his private telephone number, so I could call him for more discussion later, which I did on several occasions. A minister's son who has had his own share of tragedy as well as great success, Art Linkletter has continued to express undiminished interest in the problems of drug abuse throughout the world. It was a real inspiration to talk to him.

More and more, I wanted to step out into my own ministry, but I just didn't have the nerve to let go of my job at the Chapel. I simply did not trust God enough to take that big a step of faith. So I stayed on, and the Lord continued to teach me things I needed to know, while my faith built up.

Finally, when we set up the Christmas tree lot the second year, 1972, I began to think I must be Santa Claus, so busy was I cutting trees and flocking them and doing everything there was to do around that place. I prayed hard for the Lord to give me patience, because while I was happy in His service, I was in and out of the Chapel at the time, preaching on the side whenever I could, and it was beginning to bother me, being stretched in so many directions.

Finally, I called June Duncan to talk to her about the ministry at the Chapel. I liked to rap with her because she had a down-to-earth understanding of what was going on, and wasn't one to waste words. "I want to tell you something Gary, now that you've brought it up," she said. "You have to either get on or get off. Make up your mind: either go into evangelism full time, or else put it out of your mind and come into the church all the way and quit traveling around!"

Over my shoulder, while I was talking with June, I could hear Satan making sneering remarks. "Why, you stupid jerk," he was saying, "how can you go out into the ministry with only a hundred bucks in your pocket? Why, you'll have to make close to seven hundred and fifty a month just to keep up with your bills . . . the house payment, the car payment, that extra loan you took out, the phone, the lights and gas, food — how about gas for the car? — to say nothing of insurance and doctor bills and clothes! And there won't be any money coming in at all!"

I was tempted to listen; in fact, I nearly gave in. But I didn't. I had to use my faith in God, to step out on that faith.

"June," I said, "you're right. It isn't fair to the Chapel to go on the way I've been doing. I'm giving notice now that I'm going on my own." I paused, as the full meaning of what I had just said sank home. "I hope you'll pray for me."

"We will, Gary, we will! God bless you!"

I finished the day in the Christmas tree lot without really knowing what I was doing. I'd taken the big step. I thought about some of the good things that had happened in my ministry . . . and some of the bad. I had no idea what to expect.

"Lord," I prayed, "all I can do is put it in Your hands." Then I hurried home to Nanell with the news. We'd soon be on our own.

Would the Holy Spirit come through? I wondered.

Chapter Nineteen

It wasn't all that easy to step out on faith, but I knew it had to be done, and Nanell was with me all the way. Making it even more of a leaning on the Lord, our prayers for a baby had been answered, so our responsibilities were due to get heavier within a short time.

We'd wanted a child so badly that we'd gotten on our knees to pray that God would bless us with one. There was Nanell, praying for a little girl. But at the same time, I was busy praying for a little boy.

"Honey, we'd better get it together," I said to her. And so we did . . . we both prayed for a little boy, and our prayers were answered with the arrival of Shane, who is three years old at the time of this writing. Truly the blessings of the Lord are marvelous to behold!

The first month of my independent ministry, I made only $293 — a long way from meeting the needs of our everyday lives. Had I blown it again? Was my evangelism to be a failure? I thought about some of the events that had led me to go on my own.

There was the Solid Rock Coffee House in Sylmar (a community just north of Los Angeles) — Mom Bean's place. I went there to preach and I wasn't sure how it was all going to work out. Mom and the kids who knew her got busy and cleaned up a large field and built a stage and all the other necessary things so we could conduct the meeting. The first night there I was sick, but I knew God wanted me to preach, and it was a real thrill to see about two hundred and fifty people sitting in those chairs waiting to hear the message of God's love. That night, and each night throughout the series of meetings, there were from sixty to seventy kids lined up for salvation, waiting for God to heal their bodies and fill them with the Holy Spirit.

The success of the revival led to establishing a new coffee house, with another house behind it. At Mom Bean's request I became the Chaplain of that coffee house, and I've preached there at the Solid Rock off and on for more than three years. I began to realize, more than ever before, the fantastic ways in which God works through us — his earthly servants.

A young woman by the name of Pat Palmer kept coming to the meetings and had a real burden. "Please pray for my husband," she said. "I feel certain God's going to save Bob; but will you pray for him?" So we prayed for her husband, many times, and finally he showed up at one of the meetings. He'd just come from a wedding where he'd been taking pictures.

"Okay if I take some pictures of you?" he asked.

"Sure, I can use them in my ministry."

So he took some photos, and a few nights later he was back again, but by the time the service was over, something had happened to him. Looking through the lens of his camera, he'd seen Jesus Christ.

"Gary, I want to be saved!" he told me, and the Lord came into his life that night and he was born again. From that moment on Bob began reading the Bible, along with coming to the Solid Rock and other meetings, and he kept on taking pictures, too. Then he felt a calling to go to Bible school, and although he and Pat didn't have any money, they just stepped out on faith. Today he's in Bible school studying the Word and I know the Lord will use him as a teacher.

Another unforgettable incident at the Coffee House, and one that taught me a good lesson, occurred when I was in a hurry to get ready to go preach there, and I pulled on a pair of old corduroy slacks.

"Gary, those pants have a loose snap on them," Nanell told me. "You'd better wear something else — or at least wear a belt in case they come unsnapped."

"Oh, don't worry about it," I said. "Everything's fine." I was in a hurry and didn't want to be bothered.

From behind the pulpit I could begin to feel the inspiration of the Holy Ghost, so I moved out to the right and started going pretty heavy about how Job went through all those trials and tribulations, when all of a sudden, I felt a quick snap at my middle. Nanell had been right on!

Quickly, I leaped back behind the pulpit, hoping no one had noticed that my pants had come loose. I spread my legs as far as I could to hold them up, and kept on preaching so nobody would know I had a problem. But the louder I preached, the further down they slipped. I got the message quickly. I began to speak softer and softer, getting down to a quiet tone that finally became little more than a whisper. By then, my pants were clear down to my knees!

It was time to end the sermon, but what could I do? There had to be some way to get my pants back up without anyone seeing me do it. Along with my "still small voice" to the audience, I was breathing a prayer to God repenting for not listening to Him when He spoke to me through Nanell, and asking Him for deliverance from my dilemma. And as usual, He came through!

"I want to make a different kind of altar call tonight," I said softly. "I want everyone to stand up and turn around, face the back wall, and raise your hands — then close your eyes."

They must have thought I was a cop, ready to pull a search on them, for without hesitating, the entire audience faced the wall with their hands up in the air like they were caught in the act of burglary or something worse.

In an instant, I had retrieved my fallen pants and fastened them again. "Dear Lord," I prayed aloud, "for all thy blessings on these, thy children, we give our humble thanks. Touch our hearts tonight, and lead us in thy ways, oh Lord, forever! Amen." And I told them to turn around, inviting those who wanted to give their lives to God to seek the salvation of His Son at the altar.

Afterward, several people came up to me with a simple message. "Gary, that was the most fantastic sermon I ever

heard," one girl said. "I've never heard you speak so softly."
She smiled. "You really should do that more often."

* * * *

Faced with a far more serious problem with only $293 coming
in that first month of independent evangelism, I cried out to
God. "Lord!" I yelled. "Help us! We can't make it this way!"

I should have known better than to doubt, even for an
instant. I was called up the California coast to Santa Barbara for
a two-week period, and the church people from where I was to
speak put me up in a motel. Alone and lonely without my little
family, I sat there and wondered if, indeed, God was going to
use me. Again, I should never have questioned, for if you just
give in and let go, the Holy Spirit will move through you. Next
day, the first morning of the session, I was driving down the
street listening to the radio.

"Turn off the radio!" God's voice came to me loud and clear.

"Okay, Lord!" I said, and obeyed.

Then came a more complicated message. God told me He
was going to heal someone who had cancer, through me.

"Oh, come on, God!" I said.

But the message was still there. It was something I felt,
rather than heard. The Lord said to me, "Yes, I'm going to do
it!"

So I said, "All right, Lord — whatever you say."

I went on to the meeting that morning and preached about
His marvelous healing powers. And when I made the altar call,
there must have been anywhere from 50 to 70 people come
forward. I went up to this one big, strong-looking man. At the
time, I had no idea what was wrong with him.

"Would you pray for my stomach, Reverend Fisher?" he
asked.

So I did. I prayed for many people that morning. And I
especially asked the Lord's blessing and help for this man's
stomach.

Afterward, this same man — Bill Forsythe — asked me if I'd
like to go out to lunch with him and his family and the pastor of
the church.

I welcomed the opportunity. "Yes, I'll be happy to!"

As we were waiting at the restaurant to be seated, Bill's wife spoke to me. "Did you know that Bill has cancer?" she asked.

"You're kidding!"

"No," she said, acting sort of puzzled. "He has cancer of the stomach, and the doctors say he has no more than two or three months to live."

"Then Bill must be the one!" I murmured aloud, and noticing that she looked confused, I went on. "This morning, when I was driving to the church, God told me He was going to heal somebody of cancer. Now I believe with all my heart that He has done so, for Bill asked me to pray for his stomach. It was God's will!"

Inside the dining room, Bill's wife told him God had told me He was going to heal someone of cancer. I looked at Bill's face, and it changed from a pale white to pink, right then and there. I knew God had healed him. Three days later, he went back to his doctor, and they stuck tubes down his throat to take pictures of his stomach, to see how the cancer was developing, and whether they could do anything to help him. They'd done all they could up to that point, but the malignancy was too far advanced — Bill was sure to die soon.

Now, the pictures revealed, Bill's stomach was just like a baby's — totally clear of any problems! God had healed him, in an extraordinary, almost unbelievable way! The doctors themselves said it was a miracle.

When Bill came to the service the following Sunday, he stood up behind the pulpit and testified how God had healed him. And with tears in his eyes, he gave his testimony. It proved to me again that God indeed intended to use me, that all the struggles and abuse I went through were part of the background I needed for Him to use me in a mighty way.

There was a thrill in my heart after the Santa Barbara meetings, for I knew He had blessed my ministry. The gifts and offerings came to more than a month's expenses, plus so much meat, a gift from Bill, it took Nanell almost four hours to cut it all up and package it for freezing. We were on the mountain top, for sure!

But there are mountains to climb, and there are valleys that follow. Jesus says He will make your path straight . . . He'll bring the mountains down and the valleys up to make a straight path for the coming of the Lord. And that's how it was. A valley . . . then a mountain . . . then another valley. There came a later time when I was once again in my bedroom crying out to God. We'd been taking drug addicts off the streets, and kids that needed help, and there just wasn't enough money to stretch out and cover all the expenses. We didn't have any food in the house or any milk for the baby. Things were that rough.

"Oh, Lord!" I said. "I'm your servant. I'm a man of God who wants to be used of God, but we don't have anything in the house!" I paused, but there wasn't any lightning; there wasn't any manna dropping from heaven. "Lord, you said you'd meet our needs!" I cried out, and then I walked back and forth in my room and kept repeating. "Oh, Lord, help us! Where are you, now that we need you, Lord?"

I was walking through this valley, and the word, "walk," in the Hebrew means "to grow." It means to grow up. The thought came to me, "I'm not growing up — I'm dying!"

And right then, God said to me, "That's right — I want you to die. Except a seed fall in the ground and die, it abideth alone, but if it dies, it bringeth forth much fruit."

Many people are lonely today because they haven't allowed themselves to die in the Lord. God wants you to take up your cross and follow him. Where? To Calvary.

Well, God spoke to me at that time and said, "I'm going to be there, it's going to be all right."

About then, I heard a knock on the front door, and when I opened it, there stood Daryl Dewey with two quarts of milk and a $10 bill. He and his mother, Helen Dewey, knew us, and loved us, and here was Daryl at a real time of need.

I looked into his eyes, and all I could say was, "God sent an angel!"

These are the things that give you faith, the things that make you strong. When you're going through those valleys, there's always someone who's going to come by and help you through. You just have to depend on God, to ask Him for help, because

He will come through. But it's walking through the valleys that causes you to grow.

There was another valley we were walking through at that time also. Shane, our beloved little boy, became sick, and we didn't know what to do. We called the doctor and took him to the emergency ward of a nearby hospital. The doctors looked at him and told us he wasn't eating well, which we already knew. He was losing weight fast — dark circles were under his eyes and he was pale and listless. We didn't know what to do, so we took him to another hospital, and still there was no improvement. Finally we brought him home. He'd lost a lot of weight and was so skinny, he looked like a little skeleton.

When I looked into his eyes and saw those dark circles, I could feel my heart breaking. And right then, God spoke to me.

"Now that you've tried everything else, Gary, there's one thing you haven't tried — you, a man of God!" I racked my brain to come up with what we'd missed. "You forgot to pray for your own son!" the Lord said to me.

Without hesitating, I laid hands on my little boy, and said, "Oh, God — heal him, in the name of Jesus Christ!"

From that moment on, God began a healing in our son's life. Shane started eating again and started gaining weight. He's now a strong, healthy boy, doing all the things a three-year-old does — and that includes all the mischief he can get into to drive us half-crazy!

God brought us out of that valley and gave us more faith. And He blessed us again a short time after that when He brought Sherry into our lives. Sherry came to us as an abused nine-year-old foster child. At an early age, she and her sisters and brother were sent to live with uncaring relatives, the result of her parents' divorce. The youngsters were shuffled around from one home to another for years — always a burden on whoever was supposed to be taking care of them.

Sherry and the others were beaten, neglected, treated with little, if any, love. They were finally left at an agency for children whose parents desire to release custody. As a result, her life had been one of fear, always unsettled, with never a home she could call her own. She felt she was nothing more than an unwelcome pain in the neck to those around her. And when she came to us, she found it easier to communicate through punishment received than through the love we tried to project. She would respond to corrective words by getting sick to her stomach — the fear that we, too, would reject her was a living thing in her heart, because of the years of abuse she had endured.

But in a very short time, Sherry's love for us and our love for her triumphed, telling us that God intended her to be a permanent part of our family, too. So the Fisher family became four, as adoption procedures added our, by then, eleven-year-old daughter, Sherry Fisher.

* * * *

I was called to San Diego to preach, and out of that meeting came a contact which the Lord used to find a home for the book Bob McGrath and I had put together a couple of years before. Jean Jolley, a lady minister who was working as media director for a large religious organization there, came to hear me, and when I told her about our book, she offered to try to sell it through some of her many publishing contacts. It turned out she and Bob had also been friends for many years, so with Jean acting as our agent, our book was sold to Hawthorn Books, Inc., Publishers, of New York. We decided to call it "Satan's Been Cross Since Calvary" — a title suggested by Nanell. Bob finished up the remaining chapters, using my sermons based on nursery rhymes, fairy tales, and familiar Bible stories, and the book was published as an original paperback in spring, 1974.

Meanwhile, in San Diego one night, I was preaching about a rich man who never would share his money, and how the Lord was trying to teach him to use his money to help others. After my sermon, I was standing at the right side of the church, ministering to those who came forward to accept Jesus, and a great big man was standing there, with a beautiful necklace around his neck.

He was a giant of a man and standing there shaking from head to foot. He was holding an old, well-worn Bible, and I could see he was waiting to talk to me. Watching him, I could see the power of God all over him. And when he finally came up to me, he told me he had just sold his place in Alaska, and there was something he just had to give me.

He opened up his Bible then, and there was $500 between the pages. I'd never seen that much cash in one stack before in my life. And I suddenly realized that only the week before, God had spoken to me to give a lady we knew, Tina, $50 because she and her children were in need. When I handed her the money, she began crying.

"God meets my needs!" she said, and she was right.

Now, the $50 I'd given to help another was being returned ten-fold, as God touched this man's heart during the meeting — a man I'd never before seen in my life! It was another of His miracles, and I could hardly wait to call Nanell and share the news with her.

Another time, I knew God wanted me to give $40 to a friend, so I called him and asked him to come over, and I gave him the cash. It blew his mind — he just couldn't understand. He needed the money the worst way, but it was hard for him to believe the Lord wanted him to have it.

The incredible thing was, when I went to my next series of meetings, Ron and Janie Chapman wanted to take me out for a hamburger afterward, and when we were seated in a restaurant, Ron told me he'd wanted to loan me something, but that God had spoken to him to give it to me.

"Look under the table," Ron said.

I thought to myself, "Oh, brother, what does he want me to look under the table for?"

But I looked, and lo and behold, there was $600. God had blessed us again, for although Ron and Janie didn't know it, that was just the amount we needed to buy copies of the new book I'd written, so I could have them available wherever I preached.

The point is, God knows your needs, and if you have faith and depend on Him, He'll meet those needs! Only believe!

In a following crusade in El Cajon, a San Diego suburb, when I made the altar call many came forward for healing. Among them were a mother and father with a three-year-old boy who had been deaf since he was a tiny baby. I prayed to God to heal this little boy's ears, and the prayer was answered. God opened the boy's ears, and he could hear. He began screaming at the top of his lungs; I suppose any of us would scream if we were suddenly able to hear for the first time. What a blessing!

The Lord's lessons to us sometimes come in strange ways. In the second week of another convocation shortly after that, I lost my voice. You can imagine what that kind of problem can do to an evangelist! I said, "Oh, God, what am I going to do now?" I should never have doubted.

The Lord was simply trying to teach me about His gift of the word of knowledge, that in ministering to people, I didn't have to prepare a formal sermon where I would depend on my notes to remind me what to say. He spoke to me, and following through, I started a song service. My voice certainly wasn't strong enough to preach, but we could all share God's love through hymns of praise and thanksgiving.

And during a song, God showed me a particular man and woman sitting in a pew at my right. He told me the man's leg was badly hurt and he was soon to have surgery. The Lord's message to me was to tell the man and woman to stand up right then, and to tell the woman to lay hands on her husband, that he would be healed. She did so, and God healed his leg. What a miracle!

* * * *

And He continued to teach me about money. One day a man called me and asked if he could borrow $50. "Well, I'm trying to save money for a new engine, because my car just blew up," I said. I was pretty bitter about that one; I'd just finished a two-week session in Hesperia (a high desert community 150 miles northeast of Los Angeles), and I'd put a new engine in my car, and then it blew up. I couldn't understand God letting this happen to me. But He reminded me that all things work together for good to them that love the Lord. So I nodded my head and had the car towed to a service station.

Now, here was this friend asking for $50! "Sorry, I just don't have it," I said, "but I'll try to get hold of someone else who might lend it to you."

No sooner had I hung up the phone than Nanell came in. I've

already pointed out that she can really listen to the voice of God.

"Why don't you just *give* him the money?" she said. "Don't lend it to him. Don't you know God wants us to give it to him? Otherwise he wouldn't have called us."

"But, Honey," I said, "we don't have it."

"Oh, yes we do," she said. "God will give it back to us."

Well, fine, but I still tried to call a few people to lend my friend the money he needed. What a silly notion! Finally God spoke to me, and this time I listened. I called my friend and told him to come over — we'd give him the money. And when we did, it really blessed his heart. He felt the power of God in his life, and it encouraged him to go on for the Lord.

I forgot about the money and went on to another meeting in El Cajon. And the first thing that happened was one young man I visited handed me a hundred dollars, "to help cover that new engine." Really a blessing!

The next week, I went to a meeting at National City, another suburb of San Diego, and a man handed me a check afterwards. Without even looking at the check, I put my arms around him and thanked him. Later, on the way home with Ron and Janie Chapman in the car, I opened up the check: $1,500! I'd never seen so much money in my life!

The Lord spoke to me then. "You see, you gave that man fifty dollars when he needed it. You loved him in My name, and now everything's going to be all right."

The incident could have ended there, but it didn't. A few days later, after we'd decided to use the money toward a much-needed new car — for Nanell and I would be going to Barstow in mid-summer and we needed air conditioning there desperately — Dave and Marilyn Woods, who'd given us the generous check, heard the Lord talking to them about covering the entire cost — not just a down payment. It was fantastic! After we'd picked out a brand new gold 1974 Ford LTD that looked like the Lord's chariot, they even turned around and bought back our old Chevy, which we'd used as a down payment, so we'd have an extra car for Nanell to use. We'd given a friend $50 when he was in need; our gift had been returned to us, with the Lord's blessing, many times over.

We drove to minister in Barstow that summer, praising God all the way. It was hard to believe what He had done in our lives, the blessings He had given. And as had happened before in other meetings, I could feel God there moving me to talk to a woman sitting on the right side of the congregation, weeping. She had blown it, she said. Her house was upside down. Her husband was packing his clothes, getting ready to leave her.

"Do you know what we're going to do?" I asked.

Her tearful eyes met mine. "No."

"I'm going to sic the Holy Ghost on him," I said. "The Holy Spirit is going to touch him right now, and when He hits him, he's going to unpack his suitcase and wait for you at home."

She just stood there, her mouth open, but I knew the power of God. "Not only that, he's going to come to the meeting with you tomorrow night," I said.

She broke down. "Dear God — I hope so!" she cried.

"You bring him here tomorrow night," I told her.

She went home, and I learned later that her husband said to her, "Honey, all I could think of was the blood of Jesus Christ. Something just came over me, and suddenly the blood of Jesus Christ was all over me. I want to stay — I want to be helped." He unpacked his suitcase, and he came to the gathering the next night, where God touched him and set him free.

That is God's power, that is the word of knowledge, that is understanding the authority of God.

When we got back home from Barstow, there was disturbing news. Louise and Percy Jones, Nanell's mother and father, were leaving for Lake Tahoe as we arrived. A long-time friend, Dave, was dying, and he had requested that I come there to bury him. There were things we had to clear up at home first, but we agreed to follow Louise and Percy as soon as possible.

Meantime, the Lord spoke to both Nanell and me. "Why don't you go up there and lay hands on this man and lead him to Jesus?" was the message. We knew how sick Dave was — he couldn't eat, couldn't even hold a spoon in his hand. He could not smell food, and when they tried to feed him, it made him even more ill. At close to 80 years old he was pretty far gone.

Were we too late?

Chapter Twenty

"Whatever is the Lord's will, that's how it will be," I told Nanell as we drove to Lake Tahoe. We settled into a motel, then went to where Dave was being cared for by Louise and Percy. Nanell went in to talk with him.

"I'm glad you came," Dave said weakly. "I don't want to be a hypocrite. I don't believe the good Lord goes for that kind of thing."

"He still loves you, Dave," Nanell told him quietly. "He'll forgive you, if you believe in Him."

Dave nodded, too weak to say anything more, and Nanell tiptoed from the room. We prayed for Dave that night, and the next day, I went in and sat down beside his bed. The others were there, too, but all of a sudden, Percy got up and walked out, and then Nanell, and then Louise. They all split, and there I was alone with this tough little guy who'd been a gambler all his life, and who used to snort cocaine pretty heavy. He weighed only about 80 pounds, but I knew from talking with Nanell's parents that here was a little dude who wouldn't take any jazz from anyone.

God told me to ask Dave if he wanted to accept Jesus, and for a moment, I hesitated. I figured this guy would jump on my head if I mentioned the Lord. But it was something I had to do.

"Dave," I said, "do you want to accept Jesus Christ as your personal Savior?"

He gave me the same statement he'd made to Nanell the day before. "Gary," he said, "I don't want to be a hypocrite."

"If you sincerely ask Christ to come into your life," I told him, "you're not being a hypocrite, because He will forgive your sins — wash you clean. He'll also heal you, Dave, because the word 'salvation' also means 'heal.' "

So Dave bowed down his head, and I reached out and held his bony little arms, and he accepted Christ into his life. I could feel the power of God go through that man, and I said, "I'm going to pray for a healing, Dave. In the name of Jesus!"

God started a healing then and there, just as He did with the lepers. And from that day forward, with the help of Louise and Percy who stayed to nurse Dave back to health, God healed his withered body. Dave began eating, walking around, fighting back with a new spirit of love in his heart. Now, he's back home again, taking care of himself, and the Jones family are likewise at home. The man we went to Lake Tahoe to bury has a new lease on life, thanks to the Lord . . . it was just like Lazarus being raised from the dead.

Let me emphasize, here and now, once more: The healings I have mentioned in this book are God's work, not mine. The healing and prophesying and setting people free of their burdens is done only by the power of God. Only because I got down on my face before God and believed in the Word of God and allowed it to become flesh in my life and because, by sheer grace and for some reason known only to Him, have I been used of God.

But no matter what you are doing, or where, or with whom, the secret to the whole thing is God. *Believe* in Him — that He is 100% in charge of whatever the situation; have faith that He *will* use you according to His purpose, even if it's only to pray; and then, *step out* on faith and trust Him.

Sometimes it isn't easy. Being human, we tend to forget that our faith and trust in God is the number one consideration in our lives. I recall a good example of how easy it is to forget.

One day Nanell went shopping at a sale where all the clothing was marked down — fifty percent off — and it was a hot day, we had no air conditioning in the car at that time, and the parking lot was jammed with cars and women running every direction trying to get to the sale before everything was gone. She had been in the car for twenty minutes furiously trying to find a parking place — you know how frustrating that can be. Finally, with her hair falling down from the heat and her makeup running down her face, she turned her car into a space and with a big sigh of relief, she said, "Thank God, I made it!"

Then, from the rear of the car, she heard a big horn blast. A lady right behind her was laying on her horn. Hot and disillusioned, Nanell leaped out of her car, pointed her finger at the woman and said, "Now you listen here! I've been driving around for twenty minutes looking for a parking place, so you just split and go find your own space!"

The woman, obviously surprised, spoke with a very soft voice. "I'm very sorry, but I saw the bumper sticker on your car that says, 'Honk if you love Jesus' and I love Jesus, so I honked my horn."

Poor Nanell, feeling an inch tall, turned back to her own car. "I'm so sorry," she said to the lady. "You can have my parking place — I'm going home!"

This incident taught Nanell two lessons: If you're going to have a bumper sticker on your car, ask God to help you live up to it. And pray to God for your own self-control — a short temper only causes problems, while a soft answer turneth away wrath. Just remember that God has a pattern for you — only have faith in Him.

There was a long time, as you've read in these pages, when I failed to trust in the Lord . . . when I failed to acknowledge Him, and the paths I took were those leading the wrong direction. But when I finally came to trust Him, and to acknowledge Him, He directed my paths in the way I should go — and I praise God for His guidance!

I sincerely hope and trust that the message of this book has been crystal clear . . . the message that the road followed by me for so many years was the wrong road, the road to ruin . . . the message that you can avoid the abuse which wasted so much of my life by accepting the Lord Jesus Christ in your life and experience the infinite joy of His presence . . . here, now. All you have to do is give your heart to Him.

Any reader requests, comments, or inquiries for speaking engagements should be directed to:

Gary Fisher
Inner-Christ Evangelism
P.O. Box 318
Cypress, California 90630

I am happy to announce that my own parents — my mother and stepfather — have been delivered from the slavery of alcoholism and are fine, upstanding citizens today. Like me, their lives have totally changed, making us a united, loving family. The alcohol-induced sickness that dominated their actions is forever behind them, and I am proud to record them as dedicated Christians, who are doing all they can to correct the evils of abuse at every level.

Gary Fisher

Appendix I

Additional Recommended Reading

(The author does not necessarily concur in all the ideas expressed in the following books — excepting the first two listed, of course — but believes they may offer worthwhile additional material related to the problems of abuse detailed in this book.)

Above all else . . . THE HOLY BIBLE

Gary Fisher with Robert L. McGrath, *Satan's Been Cross Since Calvary,* Hawthorn Books, Inc., New York, N.Y.

Watchman Nee, *The Normal Christian Life,* Christian Literature Crusade, Fort Washington, Pennsylvania.

Watchman Nee, *Sit, Walk, Stand,* Christian Literature Crusade, Fort Washington, Pa.

Bob Mumford, *Fifteen Steps Out,* Logos International, Plainfield, N.J.

Don Musgraves with Dave Balsiger, *One More Time,* Bethany Fellowship, Minneapolis, Minn.

Mike Warnke with Dave Balsiger, *The Satan Seller,* Logos International, Plainfield, N.J.

Andrae Crouch with Nina Ball, *Through It All,* Word Books, Waco, Tx.

Dr. Haim G. Ginott, *Between Parent and Child,* Avon Books, New York, N.Y.

James Dobson, Ph.D., *Dare to Discipline,* Tyndale House Publishers, Wheaton, Ill.

James Dobson, Ph.D., *Discipline with Love,* Tyndale House Publishers, Wheaton, Ill.

Cooperative Parents' Group of Palisades, California, *The Challenge of Children,* Whiteside, Inc. and William Morrow and Company, New York, N.Y.

Allen Fromme, Ph.D., *The A B C of Child Care,* Simon and Schuster, New York, N.Y.

Violet Broadribb, R.N., M.S., and Henry F. Lee, M.D., *The Modern Parents' Guide to Baby and Child Care,* J. B. Lippincott Company, Philadelphia, Pa. and New York, N.Y.

Drs. Ray E. Helfer and C. Henry Kempe, *The Battered Child,* The University of Chicago Press, Chicago, Ill.

Helen DeRosis, M.D., *Parent Power Child Power,* Bobbs-Merrill, New York, N.Y.

Herbert Brean, *How to Stop Drinking,* Henry Holt & Company, New York, N.Y.

Dr. William Madsen, *The American Alcoholic,* C.C. Thomas, Springfield, Ill.

Jessica Mitford, *Kind and Usual Punishment,* Alfred C. Knopf, Inc., New York, N.Y.

Richard Arens, *Insanity Defense,* Philosophical Library, New York, N.Y.

Calista V. Leonard, Ph.D., *Understanding and Preventing Suicide,* C.C. Thomas, Springfield, Ill.

Appendix II

Ways To Avoid Child Abuse

This book has only reported the events of one person's life and his association with abuse. It should never be regarded as a handbook on child abuse. The following points are presented by the author merely as suggestions of ways to deal with the subject.

1. Never discipline your child when you are angry. If you tend to lose your temper with your child, take it out on something else — send the child away until later when you have calmed down and can discuss the problem and/or discipline him.

2. Discipline your child at an appropriate time. If you delay, the small child may forget what he did wrong. However, with older children, correcting them in front of others may cause embarrassment and resentment. Use proper judgment in timing discipline and/or punishment.

3. Be selective in your choice of a "spanker." Some parents prefer the open hand, others a switch or a light paddle. Above all, avoid any item which could injure the child.

4. Within a reasonable time after you spank the child, show your love for him — put your arms around him, letting him know his punishment for wrongdoing is over and that he is still loved.

5. Don't overdo the punishment . . . two or three swats with your hand or your "spanker" are enough. *Never* beat a child.

6. Don't spank or punish a child repeatedly for one specific offense he has committed. One corrective action (spanking, whatever) is enough, unless the child repeats his wrongdoing and must be disciplined further for the additional offense.

7. Never lock a child in a dark room — a closet, a shed, any dark place. The resultant fear can mark him for life.

8. Never pull a child's hair; never hit him on the ears, nose, or any other area of the head . . . and never hit him with your fist.

9. If possible, talk to your child at his physical level — that is, hold your child up so his face is level with yours, or get down on the floor with him. Remember that to the child, you are a giant. Instead of looking down on him, put yourself at his level.

10. Avoid pushing your child too far, too fast, and expecting too much of him. Respect his capabilities; if he gives normal maximum effort, don't worry about lack of achievement. Fear of failure can warp a child's personality; be concerned with reasons behind the child's failure, rather than with failure itself. If the child is not making proper progress in school, remember that reduction of privileges (restricting television time, etc.) can be

more effective than any type of physical punishment, which becomes abuse in this situation.

11. Avoid continually "putting down" your children. Give them reason for self-respect by avoiding criticism of either personality or character traits. "Making fun" of them or "putting them down" will reflect in their behavior, creating problems in their relationships with others.

12. Children are molded by their parents in the home; they need guidance, with both parents participating in the strong pattern of direction you develop. Nervous parents can cause nervous children. Remember that dirty language or other improper behavior by the parents will inevitably be reflected by the children outside the home.

13. Overpermissiveness breeds problems. It is fine for your children to express opinions and to set goals, but they need your guidance in doing so. Never leave young children on their own, unsupervised; once they feel neglected, trouble will result.

14. Avoid showing favoritism for one child over another, regardless of your feelings. Let each child know he is something special in his own particular way, that each is appreciated for his own personality needs. Your love should be broad enough to encompass all individual differences, based on your recognition of those differences.

15. Don't use television as a babysitter; it does not provide sufficient mental stimulation. Read to your children; play games with them; work in other activities where they can react to and

with you, where they must think about what they'll do next. Balance television watching with other more productive pursuits.

16. Take time to listen to your child, to engage him in conversation. If you are watching television, ask him what he thinks will happen next . . . talk to him and let him know you understand him, but let him talk, too — it's a two-way street.

17. Remember that ignoring intentional minor bad behavior, often performed only to attract attention, can often eliminate it. If the child's attention-getting device doesn't work, he may abandon it.

18. Make certain your child receives proper nutrition. Snacks are fine, but not sufficient for balanced diet.

19. Keep your child as clean as possible, without overdoing it. Failure to maintain proper hygiene is an avoidable abuse.

20. Neglect in any form can become child abuse. Don't neglect immunizations. Current statistics indicate two out of five children are not being protected against polio. Neglect is also apparent in vaccinations for German measles and DPT (diphtheria-pertussis-tetanus), given as a single shot. Pre-school years are best for these immunizations. If you can't afford them, many city, county or state health departments provide free shots. Check with them!

21. Teach your child safety concerning matches, firearms, crossing streets, other common sense precautions.

22. Teach your child to be proud of his ethnic heritage. If you are part of a minority group, be proud of it. Your children will reflect your personal attitude, and if they are counseled at home to be proud of what they are, they will be better able to face any teasing or other improper behavior from other children.

23. Remember if your child doesn't have a good self-image, if he doesn't feel good about himself, he faces an uphill battle to survive successfully. Show him a good parental image, and encourage him to become self-confident by believing in himself and his ability to meet whatever challenge presents itself.

24. If your child continues to do unreasonable things, even after being disciplined, have your family physician give him a complete physical examination . . . his unusual behavior may be caused by a correctable chemical imbalance in his body. Have him checked out.

25. Remember there is no substitute for strong religious faith. The knowledge that a loving God stands ready to support and help your child can equip him to face most of life's problems. The Church and Sunday School of your choice can help implant and sustain that needed faith . . . and your child's attendance and participation should be shared by his parents.

Appendix III

How To Counsel In Child Abuse Cases

Entire books could be and have been written on this subject, and the few words offered here are intended only as a basic guide which I hope can and will be helpful.

We follow the "PULL" formula — a plan that differs somewhat from the word it becomes. The formula is really quite simple: Patience . . . Understanding . . . Love. What about the other "L"? That's just more Love — it takes a double portion and more of Love to counsel those in child abuse trouble, be they the abused youngster or the adult abuser.

Let me cite a personal example: At the time of completion of this book, Nanell and I have taken into our home a six-year-old boy — let's call him Johnny — who has been neglected and abused beyond belief. His head is still unbearably sore where his hair had been pulled and where scabs had formed from grime. His ears were infected and so filthy he screamed in pain when Nanell tried to wash them. He had cigarette burns on arms, back and buttocks; he suffered from malnutrition, and had worms; he cannot talk plainly — the result of the abuse he suffered. He jumps in fright when we awaken him at night to take him to the bathroom (trying to break the bedwetting that resulted from his previous ill treatment).

Johnny is a frightfully mixed-up youngster, but our PULL formula is gradually working. Replacing fear with love is not easy, but it is effective. And if you think it hasn't taken an infinite amount of patience and understanding to accomplish our purpose, you should try solving the problem yourself sometime.

With adults, the same formula applies. Patience to recognize the underlying problems is essential, including taking the time to listen to them, letting them get whatever is bothering them out of their system; equally important is the ability to put yourself in the place of the abuser, to understand some of the feelings such a person develops.

Remember that Jesus said, ". . .Whatsoever ye would that men should do to you, do ye even so to them." The Golden Rule applies to counseling the adult abuser, just as in many other life situations, and with patience, understanding, and a double dose of love, you can accomplish wonders.

Note that a firm hand will be required, with the adult just as with the child, but a firm hand joined with love for the individual can move mountains.

Suggest to parents in trouble and seeking help that they use the PULL formula themselves . . . that if they tend to lose their temper with a child, it is best to take it out on something else. Go kick the tires on the car; go outside or get in the car and yell to release your anger; run as fast as you can down the street; let it all out and let fatigue calm you down.

Some people keep a punching bag or a pillow handy to hit; it's surprising how effective being able to hit something you can't harm can be in releasing the pressures. We are all, unfortunately, human tea-kettles, and the steam has to escape somewhere. Just remember PULL, and don't let your steam escape on the children.

Keep in mind, too, that when there is a happy child and a happy parent, there is discipline on both sides — again, the exercise of the simple PULL formula.

If you, as a parent, feel you are dangerously close to committing child abuse, or if you know of the existence of child abuse, call your local child protection service (many communities have one), a local volunteer clinic, any local welfare agency, or as a last resort, your police department. Each community has some means to help solve this problem. Don't hesitate to use it!

And never hesitate in counseling to call on the Lord Jesus Christ for help, for He is the most ready and available source there is, and He can and does accomplish miracles . . . every day. Christ can turn a distorted life around, and there is no better answer to the problems of the world than Him. Let Him share your burden, and that burden will fall away.

Let's repeat the PULL formula: Patience — you won't get the whole job done in an hour, a day, a week; it may take quite a time. Understanding — put yourself in the abused child's shoes, realizing the terrible strain created by what has happened to him; realize that something caused the abusing adult to do what he did, and try to understand what caused such behavior.

Love — always remember some of the greatest words ever written, in the greatest book ever written: "So faith, hope, love abide, these three; but the greatest of these is love." (First Corinthians 13:13, Revised Standard Version)

About The Co-Author

Robert L. McGrath, a native of Lamar, Colorado, moved to Los Angeles in 1941. He served in the U.S. Army Air Corps in World War II, and later got an A.B. degree from Baylor University, Waco, Texas.

McGrath became continuity chief of Radio Station WACO while at Baylor, then program director of KLMR in the city of his birth.

Shifting back to Los Angeles, he got his M.A. degree from the University of Southern California, afterward working for more than ten years as office manager of a large labor union. During this time he also began a career in free-lance writing, selling articles and short stories to leading religious and inspirational magazines.

In 1961, McGrath became an account executive for a public relations-advertising agency, a position he still holds. He and his wife have three grown children and live in Cerritos, California.

OTHER MOTT MEDIA BOOKS

WHY JOHNNY CAN'T LEARN by Opal Moore
Introductions by Congressman Robert Huber and H. Edward Rowe

A thoroughly documented book detailing what's wrong with our public education system, why it's not working and where it's headed. It gives parents an understanding of how their children's faith in God may be undermined as well as why they may graduate from high school not being able to read beyond the fourth grade level. Although the author advocates Christian schools, she believes the public school can be salvaged and offers a plan of action for both parents and teachers.

HARDCOVER $5.95   SOFTCOVER TRADE $2.95

IT'S GOOD TO KNOW by Randy Bullock with Dave Balsiger
Introduction by Don Williams

The star of World Wide Pictures movie "Time to Run" and the Billy Graham film "Isn't It Good To Know" tells his own story of being a radical yippie and an organizer of the infamous Washington, D.C. May Day demonstration to shut down the Capitol. It's an emotionally moving account of what the thinking of young people was during the anti-establishment years of the late 60's and early 70's. Out of this gloom, violence and anti-everything, Randy Bullock's raised clenched fist became raised hands of praise when he discovered a Man who changed hearts. Contains 16 pictures.

HARDCOVER $5.95   SOFTCOVER TRADE $2.95

These books are available at your local bookstore or by ordering directly from Mott Media, P.O. Box 236, Milford, MI 48042.